Describing Water

By

R Read

Laugh at yourself and at life. Not in the spirit of derision or whining self-pity, but as a remedy, a miracle drug, that will ease your pain, cure your depression, and help you to put in perspective that seemingly terrible defeat... Never take yourself too seriously.

Og Mandino

Write Vs. Wrong

Skip this intro if you'd like – not all early readers thought it "fit" – but I wrote it for some silly reason, and as I pull out the file to edit, I figure why not give you the choice!

I talk an awful lot about right versus wrong. In this internet era, something someone might write may be misconstrued as right. Anyone can publish or say just about anything. Ha – including me. My version of events will most certainly vary from the account of another, depending on those who played roles in my stories, and I welcome feedback from anyone who reads a portion of what I write herein, and their viewpoint differs. Won't that be especially funny though? Say, for instance, you "see yourself" in my story? I don't mean my siblings and parents, but someone who potentially "wronged me?"

Upon first share of my story, and almost immediately after, early readers I trusted with the draft hollered "This is not funny at all." I began looking back at my little life chapters, laughed at myself, then wrote some of it down. I need to do this for me and laugh to release the pain. While I am not Katharine Hepburn or Gloria Steinem, I am RR. On my good days, I am proud to have survived a lot of what I will likely write here about wrongs.

Entrenched in a time where an orange-faced pussy grabber is in office, predators are being discovered, and sometimes tolerated, in all nooks and crannies of communities across the nation. A basic fear of the world ending from either natural disaster, nuclear war, the Mayan calendar predicting the end of the world or *Y2K*, I write today in hopes of engaging a few readers into snickering alongside my couple of stories.

I live with fear. It pops up in the form of anxiety or phobias, but I know that the subterranean guttural shit comes from decades ago. From frightening encounters where I was not in control. I have been thrown into an unknown vehicle, tossed down a flight of stairs, stalked more than once, and have been abused, physically, verbally, emotionally.

My experiences come to me very vividly on some days, and blur into "did that really ever happen" on others. Meet me on the street and you might say, "That girl has a sunny disposition." Is my bright temperament the reason I still have unwanted attention from creepy people I do not know?

That sunny disposition is me faking it. *Fake it*

'til you make it, or at least until, at fifty something, you finally decide enough is enough. I will use writing as therapy, get my system cleansed of the negative shrapnel that has lingered, and hopefully move forward a stronger individual. What doesn't kill you right? So I write.

Because I am not famous, the likelihood of this book "getting out there" is slim to none. Therefore, I am simply forcing myself to write it so I can get to that mythical place in my mind where I say, "I will write the truth, penned in black and white, then let go of the doubts and insecurities." After all, I always believed I would write a book, so why not this one?

One of my writing group pals said my humor would get me through this, so I sat down a few times and wrote outlines of the funniest stories I could still remember. That is an entirely different book, and full of "Seinfeld like" characters.

A favorite in that book of amusing tales, is a short story of Blue Shirt Guy. It's a comical memory of going camping with a guy a few years my senior. He was a near perfect stranger I met on EHarmony. That'll tell you where my life was at the time. Highly educated, over six-feet tall, a doting father, and beautiful. I am talking really handsome, so we'll call him Ken. A world traveler according to the dozen pictures of him from Africa and other exotic locales posted on his profile.

After just a few odd dinner dates, I agreed to go camping with him. Camping was not something I had ever done aside from Brownie Scout outings in backyards as a child. This was me stepping out of my comfort zone, and although mortified at the time, looking back at it now gets me laughing out loud.

He had all the gear, I was simply along for the adventure. Tent, rolled bedding, campfire equipment, the works. Imagine my surprise when I woke the first morning of the long weekend to see him applying BB crème to his face. He had hung a magnifying mirror from the inside poles of the tent and was leaning in towards it, slathering the brown cream evenly on his face, carefully blending slightly down his long neck. When our eyes met, he seemed to need to justify his actions.

"Oh, this is just sunscreen with a bit of tint to smooth my complexion," he quickly offered.

"Why of course," I replied.

I was more than five hours from my home, without the luxury of Uber or Lyft back in the day. I asked myself, "*How the heck did I get myself into this living nightmare? How might I feign sick and avoid the next two days of our cozy up north three-day weekend with Ken because I am certainly no Barbie?*"

The weekend was full of eye rolls by me and cheerful outdooring by Ken.

The happy ending came when meeting his *best friend*, Laura. She was my age, a confident self-employed female massage therapist, with quick wit and genuine warmth. We hit it off famously, giggling to ourselves about pretty boy Ken, and how incredibly odd that he would take a liking to any non-Barbie like me. Ken insisted, and Laura confirmed, that I was the first girl he had introduced to his bestie. Surely that meant something.

She and I stayed in touch. I eventually introduced her to a male co-worker at the energy company I consulted to. They hit it off and are happily married to this day. Solid proof that there are happy endings to some of my stories!

If I write the right vs. wrong in some of my stories, I often end up laughing about how wrong I have been. Like, if I had a nickel for every time a man told me I'd be real pretty if I wore a bit of makeup, put on a low-cut shirt with a push up bra, or maybe try rocking a pair of red pumps. I'd have about fifty cents. But that's not the point. Guys don't have to listen to that kind of baloney. I have happened upon more than two or three of these fellas in my lifetime. All so eager to "help me" to be pretty.

If I write about these guys being right about my potential beauty, this could eventually get a reader laughing out loud, no? They are not wrong, right?

OK fine. If that's not funny, picture me in a pair of ruby-red-spiked-high heels walking towards you. Deep dark eye shadow, classic red lipstick, and a set of Lee Press-On fingernails painted to match my lips. Let's imagine that I am wearing a black *pleather* miniskirt, fluffy fuchsia pink low-cut sweater, and a red hot lacy bra peeking out over my scrunched up saggy boobs. If you are not laughing, then you don't know me. How did you get suckered into reading this rubbish?

Chapter 1

Who do I think I am?

At fifty-some years-old, I find myself grappling with the fact that I never quite lived up to "my intended potential." What went wrong and how can I correct it? The voice inside my head continually tells me I am not worthy, and that my words don't mean a thing. Maybe I am only good at creating delicious peanut butter cookies and Rice Krispy treats (*which by the way I am very good at*). I am not a doctor, lawyer, professional baker or trade smith. Just myself, stuck here in a private struggle with "is this all I got?"

I feel like there is something more I must do, see, or write to *be something more*. I also believe it is long overdue. I have set out to write a book dozens of times over many years of outlines, ideas, personal stories of struggle, stalkers, or triumphs. You probably know some of these stories, can relate, or potentially *know some of the poor dears I am writing about.*

I wrote a book last year in attempt to speak up for injustice towards twenty-somethings, but I need to stand up for myself in order to set everything right. *That one was straight fiction, this one, hmm?*

I initially wanted to include only the tales where friends shook their heads in unison – "that is hilarious, you should write a book, Rhonda." It'd be so easy had I not burned all of my journals and notebooks over the years, thinking those flames would absolve the pain.

When I penned that first book, I sat down with an outline of me, but sidetracked and wrote about *She*. Likely, the ability to remove myself from focus, made that book much easier to compose.

That first one titled *She Too* was no literary genius, but was reaching readers with my intended message – let's work toward saving another young woman from experiencing an assault. We need to believe women who come forward, and we need to warn young people of the dangers of hazing and drugs, currently rampant on college campuses. *She Too* was not desperately marketable due to its downer content, but it is done. As of this edit, I have heard back from detectives and families in multiple states who agree that it is helpful in opening dialogue on the topic of sexual assault.

That book was the result of how angry I am that the NCAA. In particular NCAA sanctioned universities and athletic departments who are covering up the truth about rampant assaults on college campuses. It spewed out onto the laptop during my fifty-eighth try at writing *this one*. It succeeded in giving me the nudge I needed. The internal message that *I can, in fact, write a book. I did, in fact, write a book. Now get the F back, to writing, this book.*

She Too was a distraction. Anyone else ever feel like there are fourteen million reasons why you don't do the one thing you feel in your soul that you need to do? Especially if it's something you have always wanted to do. There have been legit excuses, like crashed laptops and flu epidemics, but ultimately guttural fear and worthlessness has held me back. That and the fact it could be detrimental to those around me.

Stealing a line from a movie, *I having been drowning*, desperate to get the dark stuff out of my gut, *but have been so busy describing the water* that I could sink. In this bit of narrative, I inflate my own life vest. This book, short and sweet, gets my head above water. Picture me, swimming through my very first fiction novel after getting this one done. Book three, I hope, will be much more mainstream.

The fear in printing this one, of course, is if I write intimate, personal stuff down in black and white, will the "gray areas" immediately destroy the last shreds of relationships I have with my siblings and/or parents? Will I lose a friend or two if they happen to read about who *the real me is*?

I call them gray areas, because not much in life is black and white. My father remembers my mother insisting he "beat the crap out of me," as he tosses me down the basement stairs, "to teach me a lesson." My mother, on the other hand, will tell folks that I "ran away in high school." Perspective.

It is black and white here for me now that I am writing it on to a page and I can move on. The concept of "he said and she said" really only counts if you are attempting the impossible, trying to change someone else. I need only to know my stuff, clean up my act, take responsibility for bettering my intentions and attitude.

Growing up in a house where abuse is constant, whether it be physical or verbal, is not where anyone wants to be. The way out of abuse, self-love, is easier said than done when you've been self-loathing for many years.

My memory is that at my earliest convenience, *I got the hell outta Dodge* in order to save myself. I sat sobbing in a theater seat during the movie **I, Tonya** recently. I felt a real connection with the part where she took one hand off the wheel if you will, when a boy told her she was pretty, and the car wreck of her life ensued. She just wanted out of the abusive environment she'd been living in. Don't get me wrong, she had it way worse than me – which might be the reason that she was driven to accomplish Olympic level skating, while I am simply parked in my apartment trying to feel whole.

In the movie, Tonya's mother explains it so

simply with "I made you." Right she is. But after the movie, I read an article about a line her mother used, that was cut from the original script. "Tonya always said that growing up, everyone hit her. Well, it was just a natural reaction to being around her." That about sums it up for my home life and subsequent first marriages.

Being around me caused the men in my life to want to choke, hit, or toss me to the floor. Number one and number two both had that sentiment, "she drove me to it." It explains a fair amount about who I am. The instigator or a common denominator in all of my life stories, good and bad.

Who is at fault really? A boy in middle-school looked my way, made me feel like I was of value. He later broke my wrist for speaking to another guy in the halls of our high school. *When you grow up in an abusive household, the abuse feels like home, duh!*

When you act out as a teenager it is difficult to

differentiate between a justifiable beating and basic discipline, e.g. using a leather belt on a child in my day. A wooden spoon hung alongside my plate at the dinner table on parmesan fish night, or any meal that included peas. I vividly remember attempting to hide the peas under my plate one evening, running to lock myself in the bathroom once I realized that clearing of plates would expose my witlessness. Heart pounding, the dread was in fact rougher than the spankings. My brain was wired to pair fear and physical pain in matters of discipline.

Discipline or abuse, this is not that book, but I will say that times are a changing. In a magazine article I read recently, Uma Thurman is quoted as saying "... stop calling people who are mean to you 'in love' with you...as little girls we are conditioned to believe that cruelty and love somehow have a connection..." I need desperately to move out of this mindset.

Four decades later, my family and friends may not understand my move across the country at fifty, or the desire to sky dive, climb or trek for three months alone. However, there comes a time in everyone's life where they realize they cannot please everyone. *Thanks Captain Obvious* I mutter to myself. But this theory is *especially* hard on mothers, because other human beings are in fact counting on you.

Plenty of naysayers wondered why I made another big move. I like to use the words of Oprah on that one, "Making a bold move is the only way to advance towards the grandest vision the universe has for you." I wanted to do something just for me. Well, that and my girls, now college graduates, are both here in California.

During my teen years I feared my parents, late teen to early twenties my boyfriends, then in my thirties, two abusive husbands. At forty I celebrated freedom from any constraints with a bunch of pals in Vegas, a good year!

When asking myself who I think I am today, survivor seems too small a word. Fighter probably fits me more appropriately because I am continually challenging the status quo. I do not take abuse lying down. I fight back, always have. That has helped and hurt my causes over the years.

The fifty and fabulous t-shirts just don't fit. Don't get me wrong, I am a small-boned person, lucky in that because I despise gyms or workouts. But absolutely nothing I wore just two short years ago fits me anymore. I simply cannot afford to continue on this current path called ME.

Out of nowhere I am suddenly all jelly-bellied, and red wine dependent. No dancing with my tribe of gal pals at the clubs, nor staying up past nine. They have a word for it, well, women have a word for it—starts with MEN, then O, followed by a pause. Saying it all together just creeps me out to the max. I feel like I am still just thirty or forty-something. My body tells me different.

The night sweats and weight gain are nothing compared to my feelings of inadequacy from inside. Who I am today is not someone who can continue on the current path. If I am to be of any use to those I care about most, I must do some curative work in these pages. Decades of feeling unworthy, ugly or sub-par needs to end with this memoir. I am worth it. My words are my truth. Predators can no longer stalk, hit or harm me, or my children, without consequences.

I know I have worth because I have met people who believe in me. I have raised two amazing daughters who are independent. No I am not normal, haphazardly trying to work out a third marriage without having recovered from the first two. Normal is no longer June and Ward Cleaver though. I am doing the work, right here, on this page. Narrative therapy being that traditional therapy and plenty of sunshine has not worked in the past.

Chapter 2

I know who I am not

A process of elimination if you will. Most days, I have no idea who I am or why that confusion, though I'm able to sort out a few details on who I am not. I remember hearing somewhere, and then repeating to my children for years, that there is a lesson to be learned in knowing who you *are not,* or where you *do not* want to be.

I moved around a lot in my twenties and told myself that the facts were becoming clearer with each move. I did not want to live in Florida at a young age surrounded by elders. Texas was not the place for me, being I was not a girly-girl into heavy makeup and high heels. Nor did I own riding boots or a horse. I moved from Michigan to Florida, Florida to Texas and then back before determining that I might need a college degree if I were ever to amount to anything.

(Old school thinking, I know, because Dell and Zuckerberg have officially proved that to be false.)

My Canadian heritage was not calling me home whatsoever. I am pretty sure that a scientist somewhere wrote that your body simply cannot go back to the Great White North once you've experienced sun and temperate climates during much of your growing up years. (I just made that up.) When I got a job in sunny southern California after college, I expected my perfect life to begin.

At about 25, Clark Davis and I moved to Burbank together, in the late eighties. Clark and I met playing racquetball in college, during that short *drunk in love* period some call *higher education*. Having just graduated college, we'd be making the jump from mild-mannered Michiganders to cool Californians, *together*. Clark was tall, strong, blond and *employed*. It simply did not get any better than that for a 20 something. Our children would be beautiful, brilliant and athletic.

Within a very short period of time, after arriving in CA, Clark began waking at 4:30 a.m. to work out with a guy who had a TV show about to be released. Paulie somebody, was mad about someone, in an upcoming sitcom. Clark began a diet of tuna (*"only white albacore packed in water please"*) with mustard in order to obtain his perfect body weight, muscle mass and tone. It was something like that. Clark adjusted to the new groovy California scene like a fish to water. I was more like a fish trying to roller skate along the beach, on the sand, as opposed to the boardwalk.

I was not at all cool, nor interested in joining a gym, getting toned or tanned. Clark quickly left me for someone I assume was pretty. A gal he met training for his new jobs as a pharmaceutical rep, good-looking was practically a prerequisite for that position, schmoozing medical professionals. I spent three solid days crying to anyone who would listen about how my life was basically *over*. We'd moved together across the country, did that not mean we were to be married and live happily ever after?

I had to find a roommate fast before I went broke trying to pay $1600 in rent on my own.

I spoke to a few pals at work, and turns out a guy knew a guy looking in the area. Eureka! Ok, so it's a male. I simply will not tell my mother. Sure it is a random friend of friend, but I cannot be picky. I know no one in the area.

Imagine my surprise when, early on a Saturday, this handsome fella rings the doorbell. He arrives with $3200 in cash and says "Okay to give you first and last month in cash, I lost my checkbook."

Breathe Rhonda, breathe. My heart raced at an unhealthy pace as I held more cash than I'd ever seen before. The guy is quite literally tall, dark-haired and handsome – driving a white Porsche tricked out with a roll bar for racing.

"Ok if I pull my car into the garage real quick?" he asked. "My buddy is out front waiting to drive me back to my old place to get my truck." *He has a truck!? For female readers I do not need to add any more adjectives about how flustered I was becoming. Woohoo! A manly man with a truck!*

"Uh, yup, garage door opener right here." He was gone just as quickly as that, and I spent the better part of the day calling all my girlfriends I'd been crying to for the past couple of weeks. "You are not going to believe this…"

By the time I came to, I realized the banks were closed and it'd be Monday before I could get all that cash to a safe place. I slid the money between the mattress and box spring, obvi, and lay there both Saturday and Sunday nights hoping to not get robbed.

The story gets muddied a bit about whether he works for Occidental Oil or goes to Occidental College, but those inescapable sparks I had pictured in my mind, did not ignite. He stayed just one or two nights in the second bedroom on an air mattress – the kind you lie on in the pool - with only a duffel bag of clothes it seemed. I was pretty worked up being in a new city with a new job and all, unable to focus on my flirting skills before he actually disappeared completely.

After about two weeks, it started to seem a little bit like he was renting just the garage, not the other bedroom. A bag or two appeared and disappeared from the garage, maybe. The duffel was still there alongside the floaty in the second bedroom, but no sign of him. Little by little it became progressively more unsettling. Then, random thug-like males began knocking on my front door asking for him. I called my buddy from work who had "hooked me up with said roomie" to voice concern.

"Pretty sure he's running from the law kid. Sorry about that." H E L L O? "But, look at it this way, you got two months to find another renter." That.

Sometime later that month, likely on the third or fourth Friday with no sign of him, a group of work pals and I gathered at Telly's. Telly Savalas owned the sports bar near my office at Ten Universal City Plaza. He'd stop by our table over happy hours, and I casually mentioned the situation to him. Just making conversation. The very next day he had a friend of his come by with a flatbed tow truck to pick up the car. He gave me his business card and hand wrote on it a number to call Telly anytime if the guy resurfaced looking for it. He never did.

Tell me it's not funny that Telly played a fixer on a television show and then came to my rescue? "Who loves ya?" he'd said when I saw him the following week and tried to thank him.

At 25 years-old, I had never been more terrified for my life, being in that apartment alone after letting the car go. Within a month, I convinced my boss that a move north to the small town of Bakersfield would be a good idea, and not because I knew anything about the place. My job at the time was to find valid locations for places my company might open up an automotive quick oil change locations. I had three lube shops cued up to begin construction in the next few months. I told myself it'd just be a six-month lease and change of scenery while once again needing to "*get outta Dodge.*"

From the frying pan into the fire they say. I rented a two bedroom apartment on White Lane in Bako, only to discover more than 100 rifles, hand guns and weapons in the Harry Potter closet below the stairs off the dining room. I had been in the place for maybe a week or two. Petrified, I called the leasing office, then the police.

Nope, I was not able to relocate to a different unit, I had signed a six-month lease. Yup, the police arrived and took the loot assuring me they'd come right out if I called, should said owner return to retrieve his or her "obviously forgotten belongings." Who forgets more than one hundred guns? Who OWNS more than..? Yikes.

Sleep eluded me in that place. Maybe it was preparing me for what would come next.

After I had been seeing a guy for about six-months, and me lease was expiring, I was thinking about moving in to his place. A favorite aspect of my job in oil sales was entertaining distributors and their clients at automobile races; a hospitality tent, barbeque, schmoozing if you will. This guy and his family owned a local track and my company sponsored a billboard there. Charming, *the nickname I gave him, having been voted "Most Eligible Bachelor Bakersfield the year before we met*, and I were "working together" a bit more than I liked to admit. We traveled well together. He was big into racing both road and mountain bikes. I'd call on customers in Central Coast cities, and he'd ride his bike all day. I was athletic, quickly hopped on a bike in attempt to impress him, and was holding my own on most of the rides he suggested.

All that riding was maybe wearing me out, I didn't feel myself for nearly a month. I needed to see a doctor about a flu bug. Quite sure it was altitude sickness from a ride at Yosemite, or a steak quesadilla meal on the coast that didn't agree with me. I had been feeling pretty crumby for a while, and began to lose weight.

I met a co-worker one spring evening at McLintock's in Pismo Beach for dinner. He went on and on about how sickly I looked, how I needed to eat more red meat. If you've ever been to that place, you know I ate almost my weight in meat and potatoes that night. I couldn't make it back to my hotel in San Luis nine miles up the road without pulling over twice to blow chunks. First I needed to find a doctor, then make an appointment, it took another month or so.

When the doctor explained how my "flu" was in fact a pregnancy, I was fourteen weeks or so along. Pregnant and not married. Me, a tequila loving, daily margaritas kind of gal; an interesting twist of fate.

Sure I had a crush on the guy, maybe I even told Noslo "I am going to marry this guy someday" in a drunken stupor a ways back, but yikes. I knew I was not cut out to be a mother. Who in their right mind would trust me with an infant when in fact I was still a child myself? He, a *most eligible bachelor* just a few months back, neither one of us were thinking wedding vows that's for sure.

Voted by my 20 something HFB gal pals as "least likely to ever settle down and get married" after that whole Clark deal, I was not equipped whatsoever. The Hot Fabulous Babes (HFB) were a raucous and rowdy batch of babes in total control of themselves, kicking butts and giving fake names at the club. I was Joanne and my phone number was two one three, and seven other random numbers. Living it up in Vegas, or at a beach rental, no one would have believed it— pregnant and barefoot in Bakersfield. That could be a country western song.

There was no way to know then how important my daughters would eventually be in keeping me alive in spite of myself.

Postpartum depression, a bit of lying, cheating and bullying by their father, move out, separated,

OMG pregnant a second time, move back in. I have for years said that I had two immaculate conceptions in as many years, but have learned how cruel that is to my beloved children. It was not that I didn't "want" them, I simply hadn't "planned" them. Huge difference.

Knowing I was not the "mothering kind," having indulged in my fair share of alcoholic beverages during both pregnancies, it is an absolute miracle these two survived. Endured, and flourished even, into strong, beautiful, self-sufficient human beings who resist the status quo. They are amazing, and have accomplished more in their twenties than I in my fifties. I still do not feel "worthy" of them. I know I am not a regular mom. Proof in the coffee mugs they buy to remind me I am a "Cool Mom" and that I am "Sorry Not Sorry."

Chapter 3

Know who you can trust

When I was a young industrialist of about fourteen years old, I vacuumed the House of Fabrics at Plymouth Mall where my mother was a store manager. It was less than a mile walk to and from. I was not quite old enough to work at Baskin Robbins yet. Goals.

I needed my own money in order to have a pair of Calvin Klein or Girbaud jeans like all the cool kids had. We were the "not haves," but honestly I don't remember that bothering me much. *Ahhhh, the feeling of having money I earned on my own to spend on what I wanted.*

Until the day I got an unwanted ride.

Walking the two blocks to work on my usual route, a day like any other, I vaguely recall the sound and smell of an overheated engine enveloping me. In an instant, I was scooped up and tossed into a large powder blue sedan. I remember my legs scraping against the ripped vinyl bench seat. Dark eyes in the windshield were daring me to move as his gloved hand swept across the hood of the car. He stared me down as he made his way to the steering wheel, jumped in on the driver's side and peeled out. I felt the acceleration rush in my chest. He was a super creepy dark-haired man who reeked of cigarettes, the gloves had the finger tips cut off. That's not the funny part.

Funny thing about it, the only true memories I have of the event are my parents and two uniformed police officers in the living room talking about how I probably made up the whole story. They seemed to be laughing to each other about how outlandish it sounded, no visible sign of torture or worse, just maybe a joy ride of sorts. I could hear them from my position at the top of the stairs.

"Golly, I'd bet that a vacuum in that place would be so clogged up with threads…"

"She probably just didn't want to go to work. Wouldn't you say?"

"I can't imagine my kid would be too thrilled about constantly stopping to unclog the roller on an industrial sized Hoover."

"We are so sorry to bother you officers. Thank you for bringing her back safe. I assure you, this will not happen again," my mother's voice sounding apologetic.

I had been driven by a crazed lunatic about three miles from those tall evergreen hedges along Nixon Road east on Plymouth Road about a mile to Green Road north to about where there is now a post office. Wait, I was the crazed lunatic. I never stopped hitting him, kicking at him and screaming for him to stop the car and let me go. Funny, not one red light on that ride.

I sort of recall passing the Bolgos Dairy where we shopped for penny candy on occasion, and I decided I was going to jump out of the car and roll into the brush just after the end of the dairy property. I kicked and screamed and hollered that I was going to jump when the guy actually pulled over with a rather crass, "Fuck you then, get out!"

Stunned, exhausted from the weight of it all, I somehow made it across Green Road into the back yard of a pal I knew, Joanie. My guess is she or her mom phoned the police, but I do not remember much about that part. The sad or tragic thing about it is that, from that moment on, I did not tell my parents about any other stalkers, creepers, police encounters or FBI investigations that I was a part of. Ever.

On the odd occasion that my mother was with me for some awkward encounter, she'd inevitably blame me. We were once on a road trip to Rhode

Island in her blue Volkswagen bug. Two random guys crashed their car in line at a toll plaza while hollering at us, and my mother said "Would you please quit trying to attract attention from men. Look what you made them do."

My mother can assure you that it's my fault that an albino creeper approached Fitz and I at LAX to ask my name or how long I'd be in town. "Travel to Los Angeles often do you?" he asked while Fitz juggled with our luggage and a wad of bright orange Halloween treat bags. We were flying home on a red eye from LA to Detroit, and sat in my mother's kitchen the next morning as he told her about the encounter.

"This guy just approached her as if I was invisible," he'd said.

"Oh, that's just Rhonda." She offered as her explanation. Meh.

Fitz is a detective. He'll tell you that it's pretty

darn peculiar how I can get a rise out of a homeless guy simply by walking past him on the streets of Boston. "Fucking cunt." Maybe he was yelling at our small female dog? I swear. I do not attempt to garner attention from creepy guys. Is this called animal magnetism, or just an assumption on the part of the creep?

Back to knowing who you can trust – trust no one. There are volumes of books on this phenomena. You only have you. Your story, my story, will only be lived by, and believed by, you or me. This I know for certain. I have learned this life lesson over and over. No one will believe you/me.

Hundreds of victims, decades of me too's, no one believes.

Predators and enablers are proficient in their ability to instill fear in others, you can count on the naysayers and bullies to tell you that you are crazy, misinformed, and delusional. How did our society get so good at turning the blind eye? How can one individual abuse dozens, maybe hundreds or thousands of victims, still no one believes the victim(s) for more than a decade? And that is the important stuff.

The silly stuff, like how I boarded an airplane for Acapulco using a ticket originally purchased for someone else, is pretty unbelievable too.

A buddy of mine from work was dumped at the altar, we'll call him Vitt. Can you imagine? I offered to accompany him, platonically, on the all-inclusive honeymoon vacation and he accepted! It was back in the day when airline tickets could be changed, travel agents managed bookings with a smile and a nominal fee for such alterations. Can you believe that I met Quiet Riot on that trip? I lost old Vitt in a dark and zany disco on our first night there. He was ticked off, sure, but once we hit the after party with the band, all was forgiven. It was that same trip where I met Joe Montana.

How can I even prove that I met Joe Montana, aside from describing the memory so vividly herein? He said hello. Looked me in the eye and said hello, not hi, hey or how are ya. It was quite memorable for me, less so for him. The red Dolfin swim shorts, tanned toned bod and an incredible bright white, kind and acquiescent smile – aimed at me. Oh, and his hands. They reached from top to bottom of the floating platform at Las Brisas with ease. I can see his hands when I close my eyes and remember the encounter. All of four, possibly five seconds in time. From that moment on my undying love for John Anderson and the Green Bay Packers was replaced by effervescent and hunky Joe's Niners. I was in an Uber pool ride in SF last month when a guy mentioned Joe lives in a potentially dangerous high rise; possibly sinking, and unstable in an earthquake. *Holy shit! I really ought to reach out.* Point is, no one will believe me, so why tell?

I trusted my first husband, enough to marry him even.

When you see a movie that has a domestic violence scene or two, let me assure you these incidents play out on screen much the same way in real life. It begins with a disagreement, quite often where the *she* says something that gets the *he* fired up. There is often a chase scene up or down a flight of stairs. In our first apartment together were two short flights because we lived in a tri level condo.

One instance I can recall vividly, furor is building in him as I try to run upstairs to the bedroom. The exertion used in trying to get to a safe room and shut myself in, has me winded and less able to fight back. He slaps me. I have obviously said something to offend him, my one liners can be triggers to men, but do not remain as that big of a deal in my head, because I cannot tell any of them to you here.

Another time, I was in the upstairs bedroom, when first I tried to lock the bathroom door, but it was a Jack and Jill set up with a slider and a door. I couldn't get the hooky-do from the pocket door quick enough. Once I break free of his grab, head two flights down, I realize the same as with hiking, down is tougher on the body than up. I fall and do my own damage with that one.

Any time that I am trying to get away, Charming is doing everything in his power to stop me. He'd grab for an article of clothing which I could usually break free from, but when he gets a hold of my hair, it's tougher. There is a blow from the initial take down. A push across the kitchen came with being slammed, either ribs against the tall ceramic tile counter, or my head against the handle of the over the stove microwave. I recall plenty of bruises at about my hip bone, where a hard door handle leaves a deeper bruise. He had two doors with those antique crystal glass handles and boy do they leave a mark.

The first choke hold I vividly recall involved a relatively soft fall onto a pile of dirty clothes in the second bedroom. He was on top of me with both hands around my neck, squeezing tight enough that I gasped for air. This particular move leaves dark marks just below both ears. When he let go, I took a bit to regain full air, and said a little prayer of thanks up above. I hadn't been to church in years. There were some tears at this point, my body simply releasing pressure. They began slowly trickling, then ramped up to a level that got his attention. I lay as still as possible, saying another prayer that this will appeal to his softer side, and that he will relocate.

Much like in the movies, the next scene is me trying to recover, washing my face with cold water, using the safety of the locked bathroom for a moment of peace. I cannot recall getting up and going to the next room, nor do I notice blood on the clothes pile until the next day or two. A bloody nose is easy to recover from, and normally leaves no bruising, but my does it stain whites. I look in the mirror and don't recognize this weak woman.

Within a couple of hours the swollen teary eyes take a back seat to the search for a turtleneck to hide marks left by the choke hold. Thumbs had depressed into my neck hard enough to cause bruising. To lighten the mood here, I will assure you that turtlenecks were very in stylish in the early nineties.

One time on a road trip heading up US101, Charming hit me so many times from across the front seat that I pulled into a fire station. Again, like in a movie, the station appeared magically like an oasis in the dessert. My tires screeched into the gravel parking lot with enough force to cause a couple of uniformed guys to come out the front door of the sand-colored brick building. Charming took off walking back towards the highway.

Apparently I had said something in front of his pal Charlie that set him off. We'd been at a holiday party in Camarillo. I wore a blue dress with gold piping around the neck, and my favorite navy Pendleton sling back, closed-toe heels; but that's not what we were fighting about. I remember the fire fighters complimenting my outfit and offering me a cup of coffee. After my short visit, I headed back out and picked Charming up along the side of the road. He'd walked maybe a mile or two, thirty minutes tops. We were cooled to a point where we could continue the ride in silence back to Bakersfield.

The third and final time Charming caused visible damage on my body, my friends insisted that I take photos, which I hid in a small black zippered bag along with the telephone he broke when I had tried to dial 911. He had grabbed the handset from me and twisted the thing in half. I saw the twisted plastic and wondered how much force was needed to break a telephone in two. He punched a hole in the wall in the dining room and stormed out. I called the police. Thinking back, what a bad idea that was.

A patrol car zoomed into the driveway, lights and sirens blaring. Two uniformed officers pounded on my door, waking my oldest, and the neighbors of course. The officers stood just inside of my front door on the defensive, "Is your husband still here ma'am?"

"No, but he broke the kitchen phone and put a hole in the wall there."

"Is he still on the property ma'am?"

While balancing my three-year-old on my hip, I tried to explain what had happened without upsetting her. The entire time I talked she was wiping my face with her hands using a low voice of "don't cry Mommy, it's okay Mommy."

The officers explained to me how there was no proof that I in fact had not broken the phone and made the hole in the wall myself. Without anyone else present, there was not much they could do for me, they wished me well and simply needed my signature on some piece of paper that would prove they had made the visit. I put my child down to sign, anger building inside my head for having even called them.

They of course knew the bright red pace truck I was describing as the getaway vehicle, and nodded in silence to each other almost mocking me. Charming's family owned the local automobile racetrack and these officers most likely planned to toss back a few beers at the next race in honor of this stop. Back slapping and chuckling as they load back into their patrol car, I figure I have given them a decent story to tell back at the station.

As I closed the door, I saw my friends across

the street wave timidly and re-enter their home. I'd talk to them in the morning. They knew about my situation from lesser aggressive incidents where I retreated to their place with the girls in tow. How many times was I going to tell myself that this was all normal?

I turned my back to the door and slid down to a seated position, ashamed and tearing up again. My oldest was padding up the hallway with the phone from in the bedroom. "You can use this phone Mommy." That was my breaking point. My daughter was old enough to understand what had happened and I vowed the girls were not going to spend another day in this environment. The motivation to protect them finally gave me strength enough to call a locksmith first thing in the morning. I would also clean up the annihilated kitchen and dining areas in the morning.

My oldest from that day forward put on a face of "protector" and today will tell you she has always been "the mom" in our trio. Partially true. She was helpful with diapering of my then one-year-old and packing us up to go stay with friends for a day or two. When the locksmith left, I loaded us up in the brown 318i that I knew belonged to him, and drove to my friend Bates' place for a sleepover. She had two cats and a swimming pool, we'd be just fine. "Let's live here Mommy. I love cats and Bates has a pool!"

Shortly thereafter I took the oldest to the SPCA and got our first cat, assuring the clerk that my three year old daughter was four, that being a rule for adoptions at the time. No need to mention the not quite two year old at home.

Chapter 4

He says I'm pretty

I spent so many of my formative years feeling ugly, stupid and worthless because that was the norm. Every middle or high school girl with brothers is bound to have heard it daily. "You suck, I hate you, and you're ugly as sin." That was the whole ball of wax relationship between siblings back then. How awkward would it have been had they said, "Geez you sure are purty" or something of that sort. "You are so effing stupid," was more traditional. At least at my house.

There was that wooden spoon next to my plate with which to whack my bum if I didn't finish food my mother had prepared, and a leather belt thwacked at your rump if you back-talked your father. Home sweet home.

I got my first kiss in middle school behind the baseball fields "hanging out on the log" with Smith Kenny. The braces of course left me with a bloody lip and a not so sensual feeling towards making out. It was a necessary evil if you were going to make any attempt at fitting in. All that changed when Gil Benson said I was pretty.

"Rhonda, to a fine look(ing) girl, and that I'm going with, hope to see you in the summer. Luv, Gil" he penned into my yearbook. And if that's not enough proof well how about this: "Rhonda You are real pretty and would like to go with you sometime. (I hope) Love you, I mean it to. S Craig."

Right along with all that pretty talk though, were the yearbook signatures that read "...I can't put it in the yearbook cuz Gil might read this." Two of my personal favorites, "...you are not stuck up like some people say," and "I hope you come back from Canada." I mean 1978 folks, I was 13 going on 14, sneaking a pair of pants into my school bag because my mother insisted that I wear skirts or dresses like a lady. Being pretty was not something I longed for, but popular…hmm.

I fell for the very first boy that looked my way with flashing eyes or language that gave me worth. Even the slightest bit of adoration and I was "going with" Smith or Walt. What a feeling.

I had nothing to insure my worth or value until Gil called me his girl. "Good luck with Gil, but you don't need it," wrote another pal in that grade eight yearbook. I was on my way to becoming of value; only to have my parents forbid me to have a boyfriend until the age of sixteen. Tricky times.

I skipped a grade which might explain a bit of my ignorance in the beauty and body department. Basically Catholic school, along with the Catholic guilt, have had me in recovery mode since the late seventies. Parochial school math was a year ahead of public school math, or something along those lines, I took some sort of test to pass out of grade six. My neighborhood bestie was a grade older, so I was able to almost seamlessly slide from fifth to seventh. I missed sex education in that grade six curriculum though.

Who knows if that is any justification, but the ugly inside of me is omnipresent. Is that just an excuse, yes. My best guess is the sex education teacher told every student they were perfect, just the way they are. I missed all that news. It's not something that makeup or foxy clothing can erase, nor have I ever really tried. Pretty just isn't me.

Not until way later in life, having had children of your own, can you even begin to understand the need for love, and acceptance, from your immediate family. Or come to terms with the fact that those in my generation will never be good enough for our mothers. Our siblings will not likely say they are proud of us, and our dads will not morph into Ward Cleaver, but you can still try to do one better by being proud of yourself. Looking in the mirror and accepting what you see as good, or great.

Recently someone called me a helicopter mom. My response, at least I am not a *tsunami mom*. I am making every attempt to give my two children the love and acceptance I never received. Just one level healthier is really all I can ask of myself no? I already blew it by "marrying my father," their dad, but I must try my best to be both a good mother and the father I always wanted so that my girls can do one better.

A few years back in a local online news magazine, a famous author wrote an article with advice for the prom goer. In the text he used a line about going to grade nine prom with "the prettiest girl in school," referring to me. As incredibly odd as that was for me, the jabs came almost immediately from friends and family via email and text. "Prettiest girl in school huh?!" NOT. Recollection of the story makes me smile because it was mostly about him, his coat buttons being askew. It did not make me feel attractive, but I laughed.

My second husband was very expressive about how pretty, smart, sophisticated – wait that should have been a flag, I am no way near sophisticated – there were so many red flags.

I had recently moved from California to Michigan with my girls and was managing an imports shop downtown Ann Arbor. This handsome devil arrived mid-day with compliments a plenty.

"Hey there, my mother told me you were back in town." *Aw, he speaks to his mother regularly.*

"So I haven't seen you since that Thanksgiving meal at your mom's place." *The one where he was going through a divorce, so sad to not be with his five children on that day, we sat across from each other and my heart broke for him.*

I was seated next to Charming at that meal, who had been a complete nightmare about having to do a Thanksgiving with my family. At the time, I was not sure that we were nearing the end of our tumultuous two years. And even when I did decide to divorce, it took another two years of logging abusive behavior and his failing to stick to any attempt at parenting schedule, for me to legally get out of California with my girls so about four years had passed.

"You look great," he praised. In fact I had dropped a few pounds by means of recent divorce, move-away request court appearance, and trek across the country. The super stress diet.

"Gosh, thanks." *Pitter pat, pitter pat.* Oh how ridiculously quick it can happen. Hah, *thinking 'bout how people fall in love in mysterious ways, maybe it's all part of a plan.*

It simply took an invitation to watch a bit of television at his place. "Bring the girls, it's just us watching some Red Wings playoff action. My kids will love it."

I had arrived in Ann Arbor with such surety. I had a terrific loving and supportive boyfriend in Bakersfield when I left, but refused to A) *ever* marry again and B) raise my girls in California, the land of fruits and nuts. Yes, yes, we love it here now, but I wanted that genuine, unpretentious, family values Midwestern upbringing for my girls. Moving them being about the only thing I know for certain that I did right in that stretch of about twelve years.

There was an on-again off-again period in the courtship with Number Two. The brain in fact warns you of incoming horrors, but the lust can overtake smarts. I bet that's what is says in the book *Smart Women Foolish Choices* my stepfather bought me. I never had time to read it. The off times were loaded with lengthy letters and emails of undying love of me from him. I remember sharing one with a friend Sally, explaining how sometimes in life I go ahead and do for others. He seemed so darned sure that we should marry, and my girls just loved having the extended family. He was playing the part of a caring stay at home dad willing to introduce them to new things like Blimpy Burgers and bowling. I was still traveling between California and Michigan for my small business.

I had no idea what I wanted, or why, but the three of them were all in. My girls were five and seven at the time, the idea of a gaggle of siblings who could drive, had video games, and showered them with attention fueling the hype. Con man extraordinaire was working his magic. Sheesh, what was I thinking? Yes, I hear friends and family warnings ringing in my ears as I type. "We told you so!"

I was married on New Year's Eve, 1999. The one where loads of folks were filling their bathtubs with water, preparing for the end of the world, *Y2K* and all. Throw caution to the wind, live for the moment, YOLO. *Nope, that's a lie, Drake made it popular in 2011. Whatever dude!*

We married in my mother's living room; just us, the kids, immediate family and a few friends. Looking back now, only the friends who hadn't begged me to reconsider were in attendance. Hmm.

I had a friend in Bakersfield a few years earlier conned out of half her savings and then some. How could any woman be so evanescent? She had a master's degree for heaven's sake, how could that have happened to a smart woman like her. Let me say folks, it happens, imagine my foolishness?

In less than three years I went from owning a

home in Bakersfield, a condo in Ann Arbor, supporting myself via self-employment, and building a new fantastic home that would fit the burgeoning blended family of six children under one roof, to BROKE. Bankrupt. Emotionally and financially destroyed. A few of the highlights here, trying not to dwell on it, rather inform potential next female victim:

My dentist office called to talk about clearing up more than a thousand dollars in unpaid dental care. At the time I was bartering web, graphics and marketing strategies for the girls' and I's cleanings. Alarm bells went off in my head, *an unpaid bill?*

My friend Sam came by to help me do a bit of detective work on a Wednesday eve when Number Two played hockey – we had about two hours to dig – what a mess.

I wrote checks to him to pay the mortgage, it was three months past due when I found the stash of unpaid bills. Turns out he'd been cashing my checks and keeping the money. All the evidence I needed was simply hiding in plain sight, just behind the French doors to our shared office.

There were false shipping loss claims and check stubs in the thousands. We had created a company using my logo creations, sewing hats and garments for profit. He, unbeknownst to me, would receive a UPS shipment of say four dozen sweatshirts to be embroidered, sew and sell them, then file a claim with UPS saying the merchandise never arrived. This happened so many times that UPS eventually refused to deliver packages to my home address even after he had moved out.

His name was on the title to my new home, not the mortgage. He and his first wife had filed bankruptcy. In order to keep our interest rate down, I got a job as a secretary so there would be a W2 with my mortgage application, supplementing my income to make it work. I thought I had such financial savvy, keeping him off of the mortgage to get approved, whose laughing now?

I hired an attorney for $3,500 to divorce him, but he overspent me by about $100,000. He borrowed from his mother's 401K to have his attorney valuate my business, the income from my former homes, potential earnings, and misrepresentations of my assets. When a conniving lawyer gets to digging around, you might find that being married for a just few hours in a given year, any income from the sale of property in that year is due half to your ex. Male or female, does not matter, hire a private investigator if you are thinking of marrying this guy ladies, he is still out there. I had a Bakersfield home, which I sold at a loss, and an Ann Arbor condo worth less than 100K at the time. We were married less than three years and yet somehow I owed $86K plus he wanted the $104K repaid to his mother's retirement.

Midway through the two year process to divorce a man I lived with less than two years, I was forced to let go of my attorney for lack of funds. I was drowning financially trying to keep the mortgage paid, my children in shoes and clothing, and pay back over $40K in credit card debt "we" had acquired in this short time period. I hear this type thing happens to loads of women whose dead beat husbands sue for "potential earnings from a book deal," or "inherited properties to be paid to the wife." (See *Under the Tuscan Sun* movie or read dozens of on line articles about "Men's Rights" cases.)

I had my father stay in my bedroom on the weekend that Number Two was moving out. My business computer, my children's belongings, anything I cared about packed into one room for him to protect. (Let's give my father proper *HERO* props here for being willing to help me out. He had been the guy's hockey coach years earlier and agreed to help me out – it was quite an ordeal.)

Cleaned out. When the girls and I returned to the home on a Sunday evening, light fixtures and anything not too large for his new condo was gone. We cried huge crocodile tears together as my youngest pointed out that her favorite whisk for scrambling eggs was gone. Along with all of the dishes, cutlery, televisions, videos and players.

"Mommy, why does he get to keep everything? We want the boys back if he is going to take all the games. What are we supposed to play with?" Out of the mouths of babes. I was truly broken hearted over the children.

My girls and I had grown quite attached to three of his five children. I received a legal document in the mail the first week he moved, ordering me to have no contact with any of his children. Hmm.

A con man can convince even the simplest of us to believe we are valuable and worthy, desired and loved. Right up until he takes what he came for and the golden facade begins to tarnish, as the conned finds themselves duped, broke, or even worse in owing the con. The value we see in ourselves needs to come from within, have I said that already? Saying it a dozen times couldn't hurt. You must believe you have worth, believe in yourself, your story, your pledge to do the best that you can with what you have been given. Only when/if I get to the point where I see value in myself will anyone else buy in.

Chapter 5

Does he think he's witty/desirable/entitled?

There have been dozens of harassment stories in the news the past year or so. Butt ugly, ill attractive men in many cases, exposing themselves to men or women without provocation. While I get that they are men or women of power who perform these assaults, do they honestly believe their play is going to come off as desirable? I get how power can make folks believe that they are above the law, but handsome, witty or desired? ICK. It just doesn't jive.

I want to say that I am no shallow Hal, and consider beauty from the inside out when describing my tribe, but my goodness the Weinstein and Nassar types are incredibly ill attractive through and through. Does a man classify his internal and outward appearance simply by how fabulous his mother told him he was? The job title secures the fate? Movie producers can have any actor they choose, and doctors can manipulate any patient they see? If you are famous male author or radio personality women will swoon in your presence?

The drollest story I have about an encounter with an ill attractive man involves a famous radio host while working for an energy company. We are four or five people in a room talking about social media and radio sponsorship dollars. As we all stand to leave the room, this guy grabs for my electronic ID badge and yanks it the length of its give. I have to say it, *he has a face for radio.*

"How does a guy like me get a date with a gal like you?" he questions for all to hear.
My initial reaction; an aghast look towards the company president, silently saying "is this old guy freaking kidding me right now?" We are in the executive offices, penthouse floor, I am expected to "play nice" as I have done for years.

Quick on my toes with my response, "I suppose game seven is tomorrow evening at the Joe, I might be available for that date." I saw no conceivable way tickets could appear for the Red Wings game seven against the Penguins twenty four hours later in Detroit. As calmly as I can, I attempt to get the badge out of his hand before he can read my name on it.

"Well then Ms. Collins, it's a date!" He's pretty sure of himself. "I'll notify you when I get a pair of tickets and will send my car for you, say around five thirty or six tomorrow?"

It's all I can do to not unclip my badge and let the metal part snap hard against his hand. It snaps back to me.

I drove myself to the arena the next night. I was seated next to an adorable couple of Canadian guys in Penguins jerseys and actually had them walk me to my car after the game. Mr. Radio spent a great deal of time elsewhere thanking the Red Wings owners for the tickets and pointing at me from across the way. Bullet dodged, sorta.

As a strategist for many years to oil, energy, chiropractic, financial (really any industry with male CEOs or staffers), you do what you can to complete your duties, careful not to make direct eye contact with the creepers. Women are automatically the lesser force in the room regardless of title or industry. It's just pathetic, but true. Fending off unwanted advances and attention is not reserved for just movie stars or pretty people. I know this for certain.

Side note: how cute is this guy that I met that night though? Richard from Montreal: Random thought: why do men always send me pictures of themselves?

You gotta focus on the bright side; the good stuff. The funny ha-ha parts of your life story to stay afloat emotionally. Dan Harris says 10% Happier, simply by becoming more mindful and meditating a bit. Time to start meditation training, right after I finish this.

Around that same time frame, I was in Lansing with an author pal, he was receiving an award of some kind in an auditorium full of writers. Sure, books show the authors face and all, but at best in a two by three inch portrait in most cases. These folks do not have the same top of mind recognition as say a Harpo Marx, Michael Jackson, or Mario Andretti. Marx died before I was even born, but his image I can recall, well maybe I am thinking of Groucho. Point being, I knew no authors at the time, none.

At this function, my friend left me at a standing table to grab us drinks. Too quickly for him to have returned, I was grabbed from behind. I immediately felt uneasy. My mind sparked into flight mode, I turned around quickly and saw what looked like a helmet of dark black hair, a wickedly pointed nose, and eerily odd grin on a guy possibly smaller than me. The ears, I was especially creeped out by his ears. If you know me, I am not one to judge on looks alone, certainly not books by covers, but this man had quite literally clutched me without warning; disturbing.

"Excuse me?" I tried using my indoor voice, but a few folks nearby turned in response.

"Oh. Hello. You probably don't know who I am," chuckle, grin, head spun left to right assuring onlookers there was nothing to see here.

"In fact I don't." I made only one step away before he grabbed my arm, too tightly for my liking and I swiped it off.

"Allow me to introduce myself, pretty lady."

There was that word again, one of my least favorites, but how could he possibly know this. My anger and resolve to run for it increased.

I took off in the direction of the bar in search of my friend and tried to control my breathing. What the hell was that?

"Hey there you, looks like you were talking to the guest of honor, what's up? Do you know Albert Mitch?"

I swore I would never ever read an article or book written by that heinous man from that day forward. Was I wrong? He is a world renowned writer now, famous enough that I'd know his face if he showed up in my town today.

My dear friend Mona convinced me to read Magic Strings, the latest book by "Albert Mitch" last year. I loved it and bought it for a few friends who love Italy. I am not exactly laughing at my memory from that encounter, but it did get Mona laughing on the Amtrak when I told her the story of our "meeting." We both laughed. She loves his books. I am getting over it, sorta.

The point I suppose I am trying to make is, what gives a man the right to put his hands on a woman that he does not know? Does Harvey Weinstein look in the mirror and see Prince Charming and decide for himself that every woman likely wants him? To see all of him? He justified the actions over a period of twenty years by telling himself "they got what they wanted?" Did they want the part in the movie really badly, or did he force himself on most of them?

Did the MSU doctor spend 20 years with his bare fingers up inside of young girls and say to himself, "I am doing what I was trained to do at medical school?" Not just an episode or two folks, *years* of offenses is the norm for predators. They prey on underlings, threaten further harm if victims go outside of their circle of trust, and get tenured at Universities all across the land. The abuse and assault is not limited to pretty or popular, male or female, tall, short, brown, green, old or young – it's nondenominational.

I am having trouble sleeping at night with the whole hormone shift and all, but did these monsters crawl into bed with their wives and immediately begin snoring soundly? Show up to work without a hitch? Tuck in daughters or sons at bedtime figuring "they are too young to understand," and switch of the light with affection in their obviously malignant hearts?

I hear a lot about "times a changing" from the likes of technology geeks, farm to table restaurateurs, electronic communication providers, financial prophets like Bitcoin if you will. Can I count on change in the way men interact with women if I do not at least try to do my part? While I am just one, can a million women try with just some small contribution each, and create a better world for the next generation? Quite grandiose thinking on my part. I must do *something. What if everyone bravely did something?*

Chapter 6

It's always something

If you start by thinking about traditional male and female roles in our society, quite often the male is "one track minded," and the female is "a capable multi-tasker." He is often either the provider or man of the house, she chief cook and bottle washer – managerial and menial tasks about the house.

Your basic guy has job, car, food & drink, then maybe family on his daily to-do-list. Even before there were children in my life, the men in my life had priorities such as jobs, washing their car, working out, and then if there was no game or automobile race on the telly, we might spend some time together on a Saturday. My baby daddy was a bicycle enthusiast, with miles and miles to cover when not working.

Many females on the other hand are waking

before dawn to prep meals, assure everyone in the household has clean socks & underwear, all household members are to the bus stop or delivered to school timely. So many mornings I'd get the girls out the door and be justly exhausted from the ordeal.

I had a couple of husbands along the way with my two. I can count with just fingers the number of times they packed lunches, unloaded the dishwasher, drove the girls to the birthday party after purchasing and wrapping the appropriate gift.

Don't get me wrong, I have met a few of those men, I just did not have the luxury of being married to, supported by, or living with any while I was raising my girls.

My point about it always being something has more to do with the old saying about the goodnight kiss from Mom, followed by starting a load of laundry, finishing the dishes, checking the email, feeding the fish or dog and cat, paying bills, switching the laundry to the dryer, checking the fridge for potential lunches tomorrow. Nothing, fridge is bare, so a trip to the grocery store for a nice quiet hour or two of cruising aisles attempting to decide the week's menu. That is if you have a husband at home or the kids are at least 12 years of age and won't likely wake up looking for you at 10ish. Thinking back to years when frozen chicken nuggets and corn did the trick five out of seven days of the week, pizza the other two, as the glory days.

Men say goodnight and keep their word. The first two guys I married could fall asleep in a matter of seconds. I stayed single for about ten years of blissful sleeping alone – well with both girls often times snuggled in the bed with me but neither of them snored. When I tried to explain to folks that I really was happier without "that extra mouth to feed and clean up after" I would inevitably get raised eyebrows. There was only one other single mom in my girls' classrooms that I knew of. It seemed as if almost no one could imagine a life without their better half. I simply never got that *better* feeling from mine. I hear or read all the time about some husband being the rock, the foundation, the end all be all, it sounds quite nice. Cheers to you who have it!

Women of today work, cook, exercise, budget, plan, clean and worry. What to wear, are the kids keeping up with their homework, will I survive another day under the current circumstances or how can I make it better? No hobbies, book groups or pottery painting unless it's a special occasion; which of course means extra planning for a sitter and what not.

Men keep it simple. One job, one or two cars, no makeup, nylon stockings or shoes to decide on. Blue or white shirt. Doctors have it so easy, scrubs. Women docs almost always have at least a bit of mascara to apply, or a cheery piece of jewelry to brighten their patient's visits to worry about along with keeping the coat white.

It was also a bit of "always something" simply surviving in the workplace. By that I mean, ignoring the flippant comments about your outfit, hair or overall appearance, and general disrespect towards women the workplace. The late 80s and early 90s were ripe with padded expense accounts and drinking over lunch with the gang. I was in automotive oil sales with exactly zero female managed accounts. I believe we called it a "good ol' boy network" and honestly, it still exists for some.

If you had children, some clients or coworkers might suggest that you should be home raising them. When I finally left the oil company to work for myself, I joyously cut out that seven to nine hours of almost continual harassment.

I wouldn't trade my girls for anything in the world, but there has been quite a bit of judgy-smudgy tossed my way for raising them in a "non-traditional" household. My being a freelance marketing person for as long as they can remember, it's been a bit of a hodge-podge existence. Friends and family use lines like "those girls need more discipline," and one of my personal favorites, "you are not setting a good example for your girls by remaining self-employed with no plan for retirement." Some of my very best friends, and of course my mother, have been extremely critical over the years. Sure, marrying a doctor or wealthy man might have eased the judging a bit, but that simply has not been in the cards for me.

My gal pals who chose not to have children make no apology, and genuinely live completely full lives, for them. Novel idea. Ellen is one of my favorite examples of this, no need to wonder if she feels like she is missing out, she says so all the time. Another friend Noslo posts quarterly her adventures with her adoring boyfriend from unique destinations around the globe. Her life is full content and happy. Exploration and adventure seeking versus diaper duty.

Imagine the sound sleep I might get if the critic in my head, telling me I am such a lousy mother, could be silenced. Still would not trade my girls for anything, but it's always something.

I was going to take ninety days off from being a mom and friend dozens of times to clear my head and write a book, get a few things off my chest. That just is not happening, ninety minutes here and there will have to suffice. When I can steal away a few hours, and try piecing this little ditty into something legible, I eventually remember that back in the kitchen or laundry room is an unfinished batch of something. Moms know, it's always something.

You don't hear anyone griping when a dad announces he'll be out trekking, biking or taking a job in another city for a few months. My ears may have "selective hearing" because I was raised with brothers. I feel akin to men drinking late in bars, way more than to women at the spa or salon, so why can I not be a man and simply inform my people that I will be on sabbatical? I hear/see men on a regular basis announce that they'll be hiking Kilimanjaro or hunting/fishing/boys on a boy's night outing, all the time. No one bats an eyelash. Boys will be boys. This girl has wanted to be a boy on many occasions – the occasion that comes to mind immediately is the time I was told to return home for nylon stockings while employed that an oil company.

Kids these days have it so easy, right? No walking four miles uphill in the snow to school, just Uber or Lyft!

So who do I think I am to take ninety days for myself to write about some of the right versus wrong that has plagued me? There it is, that drama queen ism my mother will tell you I exhibit, using the word plague to describe my wonderful life.

Right, it's not a disease. Write it is a rife from my generation.

Who can blame the father for doing exactly what his father did? Or the mother who is "doing this for your own good," in so many stories from the 80s. One book will tell you it is child abuse, the other will say it's raising a strong youngster to understand discipline and respect their elders. Both can be right, and both have been written. Is it wrong to write? Who cares?

Chapter 7

Accepting responsibility or trying to placing blame

I would like to think that I accept responsibility for many of my own actions. I over spend. I cuss like a sailor and flip off ignorant drivers, take up two parking spots – wait no, I get so effing angry when people do that! When I hurt or offend a friend – and I am aware that I have fouled – I do try to apologize. Where I get a bit off my mark is understanding my part in attracting stalkers, homeless folks' attention, and creepy guys in the park while I have six children and another adult with me.

It is a comical story. My friend and I are at your typical summertime music in the park gig. Her two children, my two, and two additional pals in tow. This strange balding guy approaches and asks me (or us?) to dance.

"Golly, sorry, we were just leaving." I say.

"Oh come on, just one dance," he says. "What's your name anyways?"

"Joanne." I respond to him and give my friend the desperate eyes that say, *let's get outta of here,* but he persists.

"I am just sure I know you from some place Joanne."

"Sorry pal, we really have to be going."

My friend begins laughing and we hot foot away from the seats we are in to find the children playing near a fountain about a fifty yards back. The children are annoyed that we have to leave so soon. I look over my shoulder and he is still staring at us. "Chop, chop, let's move!"

As we make our way to our vehicle, I explain to her my use of the name Joanne since way back. It has been code amongst my girlfriends in my younger single days when we're out at a random place being confronted by unwanted attention. Someone introduces herself as, or calls you Joanne, you grab your coat and/or purse and dip.

This guy followed us, now a group of eight with six children aged twelve and under. It was so horrifying when he approached us head on with quick strides a block or two away from the music scene with "there you are Joanne." Just that gesture alone starts one of the youngest in our group crying, "I'm scared."

To be honest, we were all scared. Enough so that we hopped in the minivan and drove straight to my mother's place to change the vehicle we were in. The kids were convinced they saw him taking down the license plate in his quest to connect with Joanne.

The seven of us now use "Aunt Jo Jo" with belly laughs in greeting, but at the time it was a very uncomfortable situation. One that my girls and the others remember vividly; frightening then, laughable now.

Is it harassment if you don't know the guy? Am I asking for it by walking the streets of town to my post office box, or walking the dog? I recently asked a police officer to intervene when a guy who was pretending to be asleep on the sidewalk, grabbed my ankle.

He snapped at me with "Ma'am, what would you like me to do about it? Would you like to press charges?" Asshole. I did catch the name on his badge "BLOCK" and muttered to myself, *blockhead.* Lucky I didn't get arrested that day because I said it loud enough for him to hear me, oops.

This local uniformed guy by the name of Block is officially my least favorite. I wave my hot pink pepper spray at him when we pass every month or two. He has no idea who I am, or why I am forever waving a pink plastic hand held device at him, *blockhead.*

Not since my teens have I been a fan of police, yet somehow I am nearly eight years now married to a cop? In some twisted way, did I expect the unwanted attention to stop once married to a detective? If yes, it most certainly has not worked. Number three marvels at my ability to get attention from random creeps while we walk side by side through an airport, along city sidewalks, with or without a dog. I asked him yesterday if he thought I was doing something to garner this attention. His reply:

"No offense, but you really don't give much thought to your appearance these days." Touché!

If you ask me how many times I have received unwanted attention, or have been cussed out, grabbed at, or chased into a retail outlet to escape, I have lost count. My beautiful, much younger, blonde-haired blue-eyed knock out of a sister and I ducked into a yarn shop recently in downtown Denver. "What the heck was that?" she asks and is confused but followed since I had a grip on her elbow as I turned in.

I hustled her into the shop, and to the back, literally hiding behind the last row of colorful cotton and wool spools of yarn in this tiny shop, shhhing her until I could see that he turned back and left the store. Heart pounding, Spidey senses whirling. *He probably just wanted to ask for directions.* "Harmless homeless guy Rhonda, what's the big deal?" She is younger, smarter and much more courageous than I. Or has she never been assaulted?

The fact that both of my daughters and I now carry pepper spray begs the question, is it us? Rather than expect our sidewalks to be safe, we must carry personal protection devices? My oldest has been attacked and knocked to the ground while attending law school in San Francisco. Isn't one time too much? She attends law school in the Tenderloin district of the city, it is especially sketchy. Where does responsibility for one's personal safety lie? All we have is ourselves right?

It is a travesty really that she had to hear at law school orientation students simply must be vigilant, the rules of the Tenderloin are not the same as those you might be accustomed to in other parts of the city, or country. At the same time school administrators tell you that "you should know better than to walk in that area," patrons of Hastings College of the Law, the federal building, civic center, and Asian Art Museum are all places where a bit of walking is required.

The streets are littered with filthy needles and zoned out characters protected by bizarre rules of the Tenderloin. Nothing we can do about it? Carry the pepper spray. Fitz warns though, do not unload the entire cylinder of gel in any one incident, or I might get arrested for assaulting the bad guy!

We once reported a theft from our car in a Target parking lot, the three of us girls were together in Emeryville, CA. The officer on the scene scolded us for leaving anything of value in the vehicle. *Duh.* It is on us. Let the thieves and psychopaths have the streets, sidewalks, and park benches. Scold ignorant citizens for foolishly leaving their suitcases in the car when traveling to a new town for college. What was I thinking not rolling all my luggage into the retail store with me? There are nowadays broken windows in parking lots near hike entrances, along city streets, even right in your own driveway! "Nothing we can do for you ma'am, don't leave valuables in your vehicle." That.

There are websites and movements these days. End Rape on Campus dot org. Social media hashtags for me too, times up, it's on us, and end violence campaigns. Who is taking responsibility for what? Who is to blame when a University shrugs off accusations of more than one hundred young women on one campus alone? Golly, 1997 a first documented account of assault appears in print, but 2018 it becomes a news story? Are you freaking kidding me? Presidents, administrators, coaches, other doctors, athletes and adults are aware of an assault or two but geez, we must protect our reputations? I would love to see a *"time is up for cover ups"*web page.

I try to read a few articles about both sides of the story when a big case like this comes out, just to be fair. Penn State. University of Virginia. MSU…say what you want defending or persecuting the predators – young people in the year 2018 should not have to be in this position. Someone somewhere somehow should do something to protect our young people. Guns? We will march? Time to trample I say.

So getting back to who do I think I am and what am I responsible for? I write today with a heavy heart wondering if just one victim might have been saved had I spoken up for myself way back when. Assaults and bullying are on an uptick it seems, and we've added guns to the mix. My unwanted ride was incredibly tame compared to harrowing stories in the news these days.

How can we take responsibility for ourselves, and protect ourselves at the same time? Remember that if you unload the entire handful of pepper gel on the next person who encroaches your personal space, it is likely that you can be charged with a crime, should any get in his eye and do any permanent damage. Right? Wrong, but true.

How are we still talking about harassment in the workplace when women have been fighting for equality for decades? I am blown away when I read about cents on the dollar that females make as opposed to males. Simple logic can be used to figure she is likely tackling more in the eight hours than he is; being she is a multi-tasker. Can I get a right versus wrong point in here? It is only right to pay a woman the exact same salary as a man in her same position. Nothing fancy or intellectually challenging about it. It is the right thing to do folks.

Have a conversation with someone from an entirely different upbringing and you'll get the ever popular, "it isn't that bad, I make enough." Or bring up sexual assault on college campuses as being out of control and get "I mean there was a lot of drinking when I was in college but." What is all the fuss about, and why do I feel a burning desire to write about injustice? Can anything be done?

Nothing better than a sibling tell you, "I don't remember it that way," to really get you second guessing yourself. One recent comment, "this bull shit about writing to heal, what a crock!" Of course they don't get it. If they get a cut, they use Neosporin and a Band Aid, enough of the drama they'll tell you.

I got that shrug recently. My sister is twelve years younger than I and was raised by an incredibly intelligent and generous man, not our birth father. *Uhm, hello, you had a computer in your house kid. I had to take my stack of index cards uphill four miles in the snow*. I most certainly cannot expect her to have any empathy; she lived eighteen years alongside my mother telling her what a drama queen I am.

My brother also said something along those lines to me last month, "you're so dramatic Rhonda." We are only 18 months apart, but in our family, the boys were golden. Entirely different upbringing right there in the exact same dwelling. If I stop writing today there is no hope I'll get better. If I keep writing today, I face ridicule and more of what has kept me silent for many years. Pick your poison.

I got an x-ray of my arm after the "misstep and accidental fall" down the basement stairs way back when. Not broken. Get over it. Why is it I am still not over it?

I cannot help but wonder how a medical doctor can shove his ungloved fingers up the vagina of more than 150 young girls without consequences. But if I think back to that one time, when the police explained how the unwanted ride was likely in my imagination, I can see exactly how plenty of others like me were not believed.

The last time I tried to write this story, I opened with *No One Will Believe Me*. Do I even believe me? The mind is a battlefield after all. It is always something with me, and I am the common denominator.

I accept responsibility for walking as opposed to driving quite a bit but isn't that supposed to be healthy? Blaming myself for what has happened to me is painful, but feeling responsible for potentially passing this gene on to my children is excruciating. Something's gotta give.

I get it, we are the lucky ones, we live to tell. I cannot help but think about the young lady, about the same age as my girls, who was recently gunned down by a lunatic on the Embarcadero in San Francisco. She was walking, *with her father.* So unfair.

Chapter 8

Who cares what I think anyway?

I likely have already mentioned that I am nobody. While I am the mother of two incredible human beings, they are them. I am me. Stuck in the constant skirmish to find my full cup, better half, or whole happy soul. If you take a good look at me from a few feet away you can see the shape, smile, clean clothing and well-fed person you cheerfully recognize as Rhonda. I have a sunny disposition.

From my vantage point, inside of the unfulfilled me, an ugly unpleasant being resides. The sunny disposition is a hell of a lot of hard work. How many times have I heard, don't sweat the trivial things? Hell, I know better than to sit and wallow in self-pity when there are starving children in every corner of the globe. I have food, shelter, a plethora of cool clothes and jewelry, nice car, great friends. If I dare ask for "more" I will embarrass myself. Yet, here I sit typing in hope of accomplishing some level of acceptance of myself.

Why can't I simply keep my mouth shut and worry about me versus writing a story about someone else's campus sexual assault case? Why do I feel like I need to speak up against harassment and illegal cover ups on college campuses? Is it any of my business if folks around me use illegal drugs or walk their dog without a leash? Hell! If he or she choose to sleep in their car out in front of my apartment, why is it I'd have a strong desire to call the police versus bake and deliver them a lasagna or cookies? I love to bake.

It makes me feel good to deliver a meal to someone just home from the hospital or surprise the Starbucks crew with fresh baked cookies. Why am I sitting here at the HP keyboard droning on about the negatives? *Get back into the kitchen where you'll feel*

better almost immediately measuring sugar for
peanut butter cookies, I try to tell myself.

Who do I think I am, and why am I writing whatever it is this is becoming? Day one I had myself convinced I needed to write a humorous story about some of my life's engaging situations. I was quickly informed that none of this is funny. My round one readers were seeing pain in the black and white draft I had initially shared.

Can you begin to see where I might be coming from on being down on myself if I cannot make my readers laugh? For cripes sake, this is only supposed to be for me, to get a few things off of my chest and move on already. Why the second guessing? Why even tell people to leave me alone, I am writing a book? So brilliant.

Who really cares that our country is being led by a first class male chauvinist pig who has lied, cheated, and bankrupted more than a handful of companies? I am Canadian. I for sure should not care, and do not vote, until it directly affects my family and me.

The oldest and I traveled out of the country over her last spring break as a student. It was a few months after the Big D took office, and there was plenty of scuttlebutt about illegal aliens, border crossing, walls and new rules coming soon. Imagine my frame of mind when the New Jersey border authority decided my resident alien green card needed additional vetting and I was escorted to a holding room. We missed our connecting flight to California, and spent about ninety minutes not being able to communicate about next steps. I cried. So dramatic that I am.

I had to wait to be escorted by an armed guard to the detention center. Ooh, sounds like fun. I instructed my daughter to go on ahead without me, but my stomach rumbled with fear over being separated in this grimy unchartered territory. Being alone with a man wearing a holster and gun really creeps me out. I saw the movie "Crash." Take a moment, roll your eyes and murmur, *"Oh please."*

Then ask yourself if you watched any episodes of "World News Tonight" during the first few months of orange face's presidency. If you did, you can maybe muster a bit of compassion, knowing that innocent people were being harassed by airport personnel who really had no idea what the rules even were. Children housed in cages because of their parents' actions? Thank heavens mine are now grown and can pretend they are not with me at customs check points.

Pat downs and fondling are the out in the open or public irritation. I was headed into a more private space. Ok, ok. So nothing happened aside from us scrambling to find one another without being able to use my cell phone, missing our connection, rebooking and getting in a few hours later than anticipated.

When we are around the dinner table laughing about airport security and TSA agents, we get to wondering what most of these folks did for employment before 911. I should google that. Mall cop, dog walker, brain surgeon? Can I get back to you on that?

Did I cry to be dramatic, or was I maybe just a bit exhausted with the long flight and time zone difference? Matters not. My mind raced around the idea that the room I was in was nearly full with male inhabitants and no toilet. One sign read, "Stay seated until you are called for by a Homeland Security Agent." Another couple boldly read, "No Cell Phone Use Allowed."

I had never been in an airport holding room, but my children had. That thought got me crying a bit deeper in my seat. Those poor girls in a room full of other unaccompanied minors at LAX, reminding myself to hug them a bit tighter should I survive this and ever see them again. Drama, drama, drama. At my age, a toilet every two hours could be considered a life or death matter, no?

Who cares what I think about anything; I am an alien after all. Illegal alien on the days when the government announces that "permanent resident alien cards are not acceptable any longer," because mine is almost 35-years-old. It has no magnetic swipe-ability, no chip, and no expiration date. In 1982, when it was issued, we did not have all this fancy shmancy stuff. When I get lucky, like on the next trip in and out of the US with my youngest, the border agent is stoned out of his mind and simply asks me, "What's the expiration date on this thing?" I lie.

(Note to self, if this ever gets out past your HP laptop, delete that or an ICE agent could appear in my doorway at a most inopportune time.)

I feel a bit like I have to care because someone

needs to start caring before we all fall deep into a coma of complacency. No one cares what I think, or he thinks, or she thinks. But could we collectively create change by all speaking up about what is wrong with the current regime? Lying is wrong. Cheating is wrong. Bullying is wrong. Adultery is wrong.

Why is it, if you are in a relationship and begin to feel desire for another person, you cannot simply wait until you have left your current partner to indulge? Ninety days says Steve Harvey; wait 90 days to consummate the relationship – plenty of time to communicate your intended alteration of that vow you took.

Tell the truth. Choose kindness. Do the Right Thing. That's already been written. Right?

When did telling the truth become the wrong thing to do? Not little white lies like you think my haircut looks terrific, but the deep dark ones like "she wanted it," when you clearly heard her say "STOP,

GET OFF OF ME, NO, DON'T AND NO, NO, NO"

over and over and over.

Chapter 9

It happened to me, and I am nobody

So, why do I think writing my story will help or heal any one besides myself? Anne, my writing coach, says I have to write it. Writing it hurts. My story is unique to me, but I get the feeling after reading and writing some of it that the story is every woman's.

I turned on the television recently to watch an evening drama about singer songwriters, and the main female character confesses she has a stalker. He just wants to talk to her. She understands him (in his mind) and means her no harm. It's a scary scene in her office that causes me to shift my position on the couch in the comfort of my own home. This is just a television show I tell myself, but my mind races back to a man who stalked me in Bakersfield.

Reminder, I am no body. Why did it happen

to me? Why has it happened to me more than once? Why do I have to cry watching the telly, think about my story, cry tears for my 20 and 30 something self? My 50-something self is still carrying that load. Will writing about it help me to let it go? *Did it really even happen if my family and friends never heard about it?* I asked my mother about that first time I had an incident involving the police. She vaguely remembers a couple of uniforms in the living room but not the exact reason why.

I know for sure that a former FBI agent visited with me when it seemed as though I might have a stalker in my office late at night in the early 90s. I had been asking plant security for months about items missing in my office, which was in a unit just outside of an oil refinery. Not until the bad guy used the telephone in my chair, making the offense a sort of federal crime or harassment, did things get interesting enough to warrant a case being opened by corporate security.

My favorite picture was gone from the wall, pens were missing or moved from where I left them in the drawer, and promotional items were stolen. Most of that could be explained by the fact that I was in sales and Texaco collectibles were in high demand. But I had a feeling it was something more than just theft. For the most part, I got a bunch of eye rolls from the fellas, but my best friend, and bad ass female, Bates, was in gasoline sales and had served in the navy with a few stories of her own.

I called her to my office one morning when I came in to crusty white stuff on my desk and chair, and a message on my phone. Seems this night shift employee used my phone to call my answering machine. Those of you old enough will remember the multiple line phones in the office. He was taking care of himself to the sound of my voice. Ew, ew, ew is right!

I recently asked Fitz to check California police logs for me from the 90s. I tell him that I cannot remember anything other than the last name, which is Rodriquez. Wait, Ramirez, well something like that. He kindly pretends to try looking up stalkers in Bakersfield on his tablet. That's when I remember that I asked for my name to not be in the report. A lot of good that does when the stalker knows exactly who I am and where I live. The bad guy eventually admitted to parking in my neighborhood and watching the girls and me playing out in the front yard during daylight hours. He worked the night shift. How lucky are we that he never stopped in for tea?

It was not my fault. Whether it was an abusive relationship or a stalker, I am not crazy. I did not (do not) deserve this baloney.

I hung a piece of artwork called 'Shattered' in my apartment last year. I am back on the couch watching that same show about Rayna and her stalker, and I have to turn it off before the end because my mind zooms to *maybe I live with a stalker who insists on watching this with me.* He talks incessantly about "Rhonda Read, this cute chick" he knew 30 some years ago who supposedly "showed him a picture from a modeling gig." I honestly did not think I showed that to *anyone*, it's been hidden in a box, away from eyes since the early 80s.

I surely have not seen it, but he describes it for me, the Kodak envelope it came in. He tells me he has seen the photographers card, and a short note of "congratulations, you'll be December, your birth month" or something along those lines. At this point, I am moderately concerned that he is a creeper / stalker *and I am married to him*, but he's a good guy. Does anyone recall an episode or two of 20/20 where the guy was a cop, therefore more skilled at covering his tracks? Go ahead, tell me I am cracked.

I am only me. No one. Nobody. In my current state of unsettled being, I long for a simpler life. Why can't I just live alone with a few extra bucks in my pocket for travel and my girls? Am I staying married to him in order to have my rent paid, therefore affording to write about this stuff, burn it, and then move on? Will I get better if I get this out? It is truly monstrous to think this thought out loud or onto this page. Can I print and burn like in the old days and let it all go? Please?

I am not that cute and do not wear push up bras and low cut shirts, so, "Why me?" Why am I crying today about some ass hole who earlier shattered the glass on my picture in early 1993? He was a freak stalker loser asshole, and I only had maybe two conversations with him so why do I care today? Did I not process or get the right counseling?

Will the police say again and again that women all across the country are crazy and making up stories of stalkers and rapists? When will there be peace? Calm? Decency? Will I ever stop crying now that the flood gate of dealing / writing is upon me? Will I allow my girls to live their own lives – get mugged in San Francisco and deal with it? Get heckled and whistled at and objectified by perfect strangers because that is simply our world today? Not cool. Not okay. Who will speak up? How can we make real change?

So many people have been or are abused that it is now part of the fabric of life? That's cotton for fucks sake -- the fabric of our lives -- not abuse and stalkers and predators running amok.

If I challenge myself to finish this story, can I make a difference? Is it going to help some young lady who gets tossed into an unwanted ride tomorrow or the next day? I have a bit of an ego but not that large. I am, however, well-intentioned and push on, compelled by the feeling that *I must do something.*

Almost every time I hear from someone who read that first book I wrote, I listen to their versions of me too, she too, or he too. Girlfriends all have at least one nightmare story. Yesterday, Nosliw had three. When I reflect on their stories, two common themes appear. 1. No one believed them and 2. They continue at our age (30 – 70 years old) to ask "why me" or ruminate about what they could have done differently to have not been sexually harassed, touched, scared, or assaulted.

Guy friends remember that one case where they felt hopeless in resolving the misconduct. A retired Ann Arbor policeman wrote to me recently about the cases that still haunt him. He veered off and began talking about the grand scale of cover-ups at one of our beloved universities. My book *She Too* talked briefly about who can be held responsible for doing the right thing, and how each department of a company or college simply shovels a case to the next desk.

University personnel are required reporters. If or when they report, police are often times stalled because the victim will not come forward. What right minded female would come forward for further harassment and ridicule, as has been the case for decades? Shame the victim. I now know that a female coach shamed a victim into not reporting. There is nothing I can do about it aside from write it here, release the hurt, move on to stories that are maybe more upbeat?

Reports come in to either campus or local police and inevitably go unsolved for a myriad of reasons. Number one, police are warned not to simply believe she over he, they are looking for evidence. Number two, victims almost always retreated after a day or two and decide to not press charges when the shaming and bullying kick in on social media. Three, when drugs or alcohol are involved, the story is muddied. Date rape drugs stay in the system for days. A female victim immediately knows she has been violated, but it is two or three days before she can remember much. The moment her story changes her credibility is questioned and another one bites the dust.

Victims quash the entire episode as best they can, and try to get back to their daily routines as quickly as possible. I know that suppression, and I am here to tell you it is not healthy. For all of the ruined relationships and consequential counseling sessions that followed, I never ever mentioned my guttural distaste for the male species.

Did I fear male violent tendencies as a result of living in an abusive household? Duh. Was I fearful of male encounters, even the harmless ones, because of my unwanted ride, stalker instances, and assault experiences? Uhm, yes. Did I continue to unconsciously choose an abusive male as a partner because it felt "normal?" When someone is nice, or uses that dreaded word trigger word "pretty," I cringe inside.

I spent many hours in therapy with folks I felt saved my life during suicidal times. Yes, we all have those days. It seems like the easy road, until you take stock of those you will harm by leaving them. Even after having children that thought entered my damaged brain.

The first counselor I saw made it clear to me that the man I married would not change. LOL. If he was hitting me in response to *anything* I had done or said, it was a characteristic that belonged solely to him. Still, I went back, because he apologized, and because I was so naïve. This is not a malady with a simple cure or pharmaceutical fix. It takes years, possibly a lifetime, of doing the hard work and getting to the root of the problem.

I am trying to take care of me, being

responsible for my actions. I hope to put my children in position to do better with their choices. It is not a pleasant endeavor filing for divorce, separating your children from their birth father. Sometimes it is the right thing to do. For all of the wrong choices I have made in this lifetime, one right choice was getting my girls out of the caustic environment I was in with their father and surrounding them with healthy loving families.

Doing the work to overcome the feeling that I deserved the broken wrist, choke out, and toss aside was not easy while raising two children as a single mother. I am giving myself a break. It has taken until now to do this bit of writing and releasing. I did the best I could with the means I had.

Healing me – maybe this is all just a journal. Shattered glass hanging above my couch. Full circle I ask myself? All this crying, is it a genetic thing from my Grandpa Guy or years of sweeping real feelings under the carpet? Can my girls please not marry

abusive men?

Chapter 10

Fear has immobilized me for as long as I can remember

Shall I continue on my rant even though there is nothing to see here? Fear is on the inside. There is nothing to read here. A damaged, torn, and scarred fifty something with no visible mark or deadly outcomes. The lucky one lives in Alice Sebold's book by the same name.

Fear in the form of hurt, tears, shattered glass. What did I do to deserve some creep coming into my office after hours, leaving the aura of fear behind to welcome me upon my return? It was a palpable feeling and, until he was caught, I beat myself up about my "irrational fear." Turns out it was not unfounded.

Authorities eventually raided his apartment

and found my favorite office picture hanging above the couch, the glass shattered in the center from what looked like a punch. How many of us lucky "nobodies" meet a former FBI agent at their office? "Plenty," you might say. "Put my big girl panties on and deal with it," you might say. Only if you have known true raucous fright could you possibly get it.

The bad guy from Texaco went to jail for six months. My thoughts raced during that time about how I would get the heck out of town before his release. His "attraction" to me quite likely would change to "fury" toward me, no? The entire series of events seemed like madness, and I had a child to protect. "Don't be silly, Rhonda. Nothing is going to happen. You are so melodramatic." Easy for number one to say, and at that time I had not yet encountered his dark side.

Recently, a friend wrote of her father suggesting she and her brother go play on the train tracks. When I read it, my mind went directly into the family room of my childhood home, hearing my father say the exact same words. She is a good writer. If only I could make my words sing like her writing does. I was so fearful of him, and rightfully so. He beat the crap out of my brothers and threw his high school hockey players against the lockers on a regular basis. It was all he knew. I honestly found it hard to imagine that his father was abusive, which might explain where it all began, but maybe it skips a generation? Maybe all Canadian men born in the 40s had to fight to survive.

My father was a force, and my mother held the wooden spoon. While I do believe in children showing a decent amount of respect for their elders, I do not believe in spanking. Never have. Wooden rulers were eventually outlawed in Catholic schools weren't they? I recently looked at a yardstick in an antique shop, measuring things did not come to top of mind.

Was I fearful of my mother -- or for my mother? Likely both.

My father, and many dads in my neighborhood growing up, hit my mother, (their wives). In front of the children. I have no fond memories of sitting on my father's lap with a story book. There were not giggles and horsey rides on backs at our house that I can recall. Mind you the abused brain does seem to be selective, and I have blanked out so much of my youth hiding under my pillow trying not to hear the loud sounds that crept under the doorway from my parents' room. Did he really kiss me on the lips with a cold sore when I was five, and is that why I still get sores when I am stressed out? Who knows?

My mother stayed twenty two years with my father. Under some lean and dicey conditions as far as I remember. There was some bit about the Catholic religion not "allowing divorce," and I suppose women in those days felt a bit more trapped than my generation. There was a virile vibe and relatively strict rules in the household. What Dad says goes, and both parents kept pretty quiet in the big scheme of things. The dinner table was for eating. Chores were assigned and adhered to.

Once per week, there'd be forced family fun night, always a bit of a scruff about what night it would be. We were going to have fun, dammit! We had to agree as a group what night it would be. If oldest had a hockey game Friday, game night would be Saturday. If my pals were going roller skating on Saturday that weekend, tough luck.

Extended family was almost entirely in Canada, too far away to gather for a simple Sunday dinner, but we spent summers up there. I never got the impression that my Grandma enjoyed the company of my mom, and there were never hugs or loving embraces that I can recall between any of them.

My mother lost her mother at age twelve. Her father died before my time, so we only had my father's parents as grands. I remember only the favorite orange jelly candies about my Grandpa. He died before I was old enough to properly appreciate his war stories. I simply cannot conjure up any of the moments depicted in magazine articles, the Norman Rockwell pages with happy families sharing and caring. That doesn't mean that there were none, just none that are coming to me as I look back and search for clues as to why I have turned out the way I am.

My mother eventually left my father, but it was after I had moved out of the house. I wonder what that tipping point was. Maybe she had stashed away enough money to rent a place of her own? Maybe she caught him cheating with a neighbor lady and she finally had had enough?

Shortly after the big move out and divorce, my mother began dating a man she'd met through her job as a medical secretary of some kind. In a crazy twist / small world story, my best friend's mother – the one I mentioned seemed to always get it worse than my mom – also met her second husband around that same time frame. The two men were partners in a medical practice, and really genuinely great guys. Happy endings for two deserving women who survived some nightmarish days.

My father once mentioned he believed the two ladies "schemed and planned this whole leaving their husbands for their boyfriends' bullshit." He held no self-awareness whatsoever in the abusive husband, father, teacher or coach department. Can ignorance honestly be an excuse for these men? All they know is keeping their women, children, student athletes in line by force?

When I take a walk, I cross the street or step into the street to avoid men so much so that I surely look like the crazy one. I carry pink pepper gel spray nowadays, and wonder if I will have the wherewithal to actually use it if need be. I look over my shoulder, behind the bushes and check my surroundings so often that my neck is *the one part of my body that does, in fact, get a regular workout.*

The mind has been studied by plenty of qualified scientists, still there is no real life "eternal sunshine or spotless mind" treatment. What I wouldn't give to erase some of my memories. I greatly dislike the saying "what doesn't kill you makes you stronger." I believe that *what* **could but doesn't** *kill you makes you crazy.*

I have an inexplicable fear of birds, it appears to have fixed upon me in my 20s. The fear of unanticipated male hands on me, unwanted attention, and sudden unsolicited touching – that feeling seems like I was born with.

Knee jerk reactions to a simple "boo" from my girls gets them laughing. For as long as I can remember, I just sort of flip out when I encounter the unexpected. I nearly hit the deck every time the girls pull off a successful scare. Absolutely ridiculous, but real. Heart rate goes up, sometimes tears fill my eyes, then laughter. I can, and do, laugh at myself most days.

Is fear genetic? Do we pass on the aggressive or abusive gene to our children? How can we break the cycle? In doing the best that I could, there were, in fact, a few times when my daughters came very close to pushing my buttons just so.

My oldest once said she would call child protective services if I laid my hands on her. I cried for me. The traditional "you have no idea kid" came out of my mouth, but in my gut was self-loathing. Would I actually ever hit my child? Not ever.

Yes, I was out of control with rage at times. Once because she said she planned to go live with her father, and another time when she told a friend she wanted to kill herself. I made her come along to watch her sister play in a field hockey game and was forced to physically load her into my mother's minivan. Not pretty. What   I considered restraining efforts on my part, received as abusive by my child. That hurts.

When I threw the hair dryer across the bathroom wall and it broke, I saw fear in my child's eyes. I have no idea what I was angry about that time, but vividly recall being alone in my room after that feeling hopeless. About two years later, a dear friend described throwing a plate on one occasion, a coffee mug into the fireplace on another. The information freed a small fraction of my guilt. I am forever grateful to Annod for sharing her truth with me. My girlfriends are precious to me.

National news coverage around that same time talked about a mother driving into a lake with her two children in the SUV and they all drown. I never had it that bad. If you are reading this, feeling any sort of way relating, call a friend.

As I write and describe the ordeals that have led me to this page, I laugh at the level of actual trauma. Yes, others have had it way worse, but my problems are real to me. Until I get a handle on the origin of my "discontent" of late, I feel like I am jammed up, underwater, holding my breath all the time. Forgiveness is the only route to core happiness, but who do I need to forgive, the assailants or myself?

Understanding the origin of my father's anger maybe would explain it? There is no stinking way I can figure him out, and will not try. I have my hands full trying to figure my own stuff.

When can we expect that predators and

abusers will take some responsibility for their actions? Hmm. It has not happened to any great extent in the past 25 years or so. Time to quit waiting for a man to apologize, take back power by trusting my intuition. He who hits, she who spews the venom, it's their stuff, not mine. The work I am doing by writing this book needs to be done. My belief is that I can be a better mother to my children if I am a healthier me.

Chapter 11

Not the marrying kind

Does the not worthy inside of me translate into unsuccessful relationships? I know there are volumes of books and self-help materials outlining the fact that, if you are not happy inside, the chances you'll find yourself in a healthy relationship is low. Take care of you, be happy with you, then you can attempt to engage in a strong partnership with someone else. Who needs to read an entire library of books to understand that you ask? Me. I read my fair share and still here I sit.

I have heard folks blame infidelity on divorce, but who in a happy place cheats on another person? And if he cheated on her with you, H E L L O? Right and wrong are clear and concise on this one ladies. Sure you can forgive him for that one time, but will things change? Breaks my heart to hear my girlfriends go on about how they need to be better wives?!?

Number one booked into a hotel room as Mister and Misses when my oldest was about three months old, without me. I was home with the baby. Hmm. His best friend called to let me in on the fact that Charming was likely at this particular marketing conference with his ex-girlfriend. He thought I might want to check into it. When I called and the hotel operator said, "Yes, Mr. and Mrs. Collins are staying with us," I nearly dropped the phone. I hung up and began packing.

He arrived home 48 hours later and began with the excuse that there must have been some kind of mistake. Deny, duck, dodge. He went on and on about how crazy I sounded, how insane I was for moving out. Ever had a person tell you that you are the crazy one? Inside you know you, but they are so very proficient in the predatory maneuvers, that you begin to believe them versus yourself?

His ex on the other hand called me directly. She needed to let me know that he might not be telling me the whole story. Her version had something to do with them having unfinished business. She simply needed closure, it was *definitely* over now, *probably*. What a gem she was/is. From what I gather, she really never did get any better and has a long history of extramarital goings on.

I had already experienced his abusive side at that point. Add in the cheating and lying, me being a strong-willed woman, surely I moved on. But, no. I was still the weak and abused shell of a human being. He was sorry, we sought counseling. Before I knew it, my second baby was on the way. Insert lyrics to the song "Feels Like Home" in here if you need more explanation than that on why I went back to him.

Not until the time he put a hole in the wall and bruised me up nice enough for Bates to get decent photos, did I find the strength to finally leave him. I brag sometimes about the fact that my mother stayed 22 years, I tolerated only 22 months, in hope that my girls can be free from "just 20 minutes of action" by any man. If I had a nickel for every time he told me he was sorry and that *it was just that I drove him to it,* I'd have about a dollar. Certainly not enough to retire on even if I had invested that dollar in the early nineties.

Yes, ladies, females cheat too, but, if you are married to a he, that is who owes you the respect of informing you prior to dipping into another well. Mutual respect yes, but ultimately respect yourself and the rest will work itself out. Some of you are laughing here because you know that I am on my third try at that institution they call marriage. No, I do not have it all figured out. Yes, I am working on me.

I mentioned that both of my exes will tell you I am crazy. How wild and crazy that husband number two was registered on Match.com with a profile header that read "Seeking Honest and Loyal." My bestie at the time was a devoted male friend and blunt person who surfed both gay and heterosexual male on-line profiles for fun. "Rhonda, you won't believe who I just saw on Match.com looking for someone honest and loyal." Incredibly satirical header.

When my friend and I did a bit of digging that Wednesday evening while number two was at his weekly hockey game, we discovered piles of unpaid bills, shut off notices, printed emails from female suitors looking for same. *How idyllic to find an honest and loyal man, I totally get why they were responding in droves.* Somewhere deep in my gut, I knew that he had conned his father out of thousands of dollars' worth of digital files just two years earlier. I also knew that he and his first wife had run up hundreds of thousands in debt before filing bankruptcy, we'd had to keep his name off the mortgage because of it. His con was well rehearsed, we were able to get his name on the title, and geez I was gullible.

Duh, if I don't love me, there is no way possible that another human being can either. Period. End of story. So maybe those two characters were not to blame for the demise of the relationships. Taking full responsibility for marrying what felt like home, of course I married abusive, lying, cheating men. My father will not likely read this, I have never seen a book in his hand. So, it's safe to proclaim he was not someone I looked up to for support, guidance, security or mentorship. Again, I should be giving my mother more credit for serving as both parents for years, but, in her own way, she served as an enabler for the continued abuse.

Which leads me to the current poor sap suckered into marrying me. Who is this cat, and why does he continue to love me if I don't love me?

When he "asks for a hug," I want to punch him in the face. Wake up buddy, I am not worth hugging. In our first year together, I clued him in on the fact that one year was all I'd last. No way would I stay two. Today is nearly eight, so you can imagine what kind of abuse he is putting up with, and must be used to from his upbringing.

I am working on it folks, he has a decent life. Reminder though, I can only work on me.

I pick at things all the time like his chewing food with his mouth open. Who cares? It is not as if my nagging is going to change him, or that he even needs to change. He should simply move on to someone who is blind or doesn't mind looking across at someone else's dinner while eating out. Eating at home, we are next to each other on a couch so it doesn't bother me as much if I don't have to look at it. Maybe we can make this work sitting side by side.

If a person's tongue literally pushes the food

forward to the opening of his or her mouth before they swallows it, can they really not help it? Is that normal? Maybe I take a minute next time I take a bite and try figuring out where the food actually goes once chewed. To the front then down the hatch? For heaven's sake, it is gross having to look at someone else's chewed food, but that falls in the category of "small stuff." It is all small stuff.

With me, the small stuff drops right into that category of "always something" which is where I am putting my efforts. Reading memoirs and stories of individuals in my midst almost immediately drops all of my stuff into the small category. I have never been jailed, pulled over or cited for drunk driving, been hospitalized for any assaults or incidents, and I am not adopted. My writing group of late is in large part adopted. They share my issues like episodes of anxiety, stomach ailments, trauma and disorders, but on a much greater scale than mine, with solid cause.

I tell myself that my problems belong to me which makes them of much greater importance to me, but here I sit laughing at the fact that I have any real issues. Still, the burning desire to write my story exists with furor.

A writing group pal's note is pinned to my wall for inspiration. It reads "you story is unique, and yet <u>every</u> woman's…you can do it!"

Chapter 11

That fiery desire to write

If only I could put my finger on the reason. I have had outlines on hard drives as far back as I have owned PCs and laptops. Where does that burning desire come from, and will this finally put the effing yearning to rest? Can writing do what seven or eight trained professionals could not do for me in years of therapy sessions? (Hint, therapists always use that line, "I cannot do the work for you, nor tell you what to do by offering advice as to whether or not you should leave him.")

Very recently, overcome with fury about sexual assault on college campuses becoming an epidemic, I was told to find myself a good therapist. Being new in town, I asked for a referral, sent an email and have not yet heard back. At 50-something, doesn't the consummate professional simply refuse us old relics, figuring if we have not figured it out on our own by now, they are not going to even try. (Insert laugh, or raised eyebrows, this might be true!) Not surprisingly, I got no reply.

Therapists over the years have both criticized and complimented me. They've said I stay in abusive relationships because I am not digging deep enough to get to the root of why *I feel I deserve the abus*e. Most said things like "there is something you are not saying in our sessions that leads me to believe that you are not ready to do the work." There has been a fair amount of accusatory, "what are you not telling me (us)?" And then my favorite back in the beginning, when I left but returned to the abusive household with a child, "talk about why you go back after getting up the nerve to move out, what draws you to his brutality?"

Not one of those self-help books said, write your own story! If you are still reading this, stop.

Right now, open a notebook, or write on a scrap piece of paper "I am a superstar because_____" then fill in the blank. If you can write just one line each day, in one year you will have a book triple the length of this one and I can *guarandamtee* you will feel healthier mentally. Narrative therapy works.

Some said "you are a brave woman, leaving the abusive relationship and attempting to raise two children on your own," but I always felt like they were side-eyeing me figuring I was a complete idiot. When I see that I am still here doing the work that needed to be done, I get what they were trying to tell me.

Women who stay in abusive households, like our mother's did, will eventually snap. Strength and determination will eventually prevail. Abusive relationships are not the best environment for children to grow up in, even if you think you are doing so many things right. You're not a victim, you are a survivor, when and if you stand up for yourself and demand respect.

In conversations with therapists, I almost always explained how much easier it was to take care of two versus three, while the label and stigma of "divorcee" was gutting me. Stay, or leave? Which would be best for the children? It was a tough decision. I would be crushing my dreams of having a happy family. If only he would not rendezvous with other women, spend a Saturday with us, not choke me against the dirty clothes pile in attempt to get me to act accordingly. I get to laughing so hard when I think about what our lives would look like had I stayed with the girls' father. May not seem funny to you, but if you were to see the two of us side by side of late, it's amusing.

Therapist number one, after nearly two years, finally convinced me that I was not going to have any luck changing the abuser. Once a cheater, always a cheater. Same goes for the physical abuser. Not surprisingly, after the apologies, it was only a matter of what next. Therapist number two rallied in couple's sessions for me to speak up in regard to my self-worth. Number three was incredibly supportive in concluding that what I suffered from was only situational depression from my lapse in judgment choosing the wrong partners time and time again.

The fourth counselor I sought advice from was about 20 years my junior. We did some laughing together. I was at a free clinic after being bankrupted by husband number two. For poor people, my new modus operandi, free meant getting five visits at no cost with a young intern or recently graduated MSW. Someone with no overbooked schedule just yet in their career.

In our first meeting, the initial reaction to her being 20-something to my 40-something, encouraged me. I convinced myself that there simply must be some new textbooks and millennial views on people like me who wound up on couches a plenty. At the second visit I cheerfully opened with, "please tell me there is a new age way to fix a hopeless romantic like me."

"Romantic? There is nothing even remotely romantic about physical abuse or conning another person out of thousands of dollars Ms. Collins." She carefully outlined how predators choose weak underlings to abuse, and that I did not appear to be weak. Good that I had gotten out of that first marriage. We moved on to how I had somehow fallen for a money grubbing conman. Her opinion being that pilfers frequently in the news in the late 90s were simply "very good at their game." Smart women make unfortunate choices while under the spell of a smooth talking, sometimes handsome devil. My step father had already gifted me the book "Smart Women, Foolish Choices." I simply never read it.

I remember that line today like it was gospel. No romance in abuse huh? I was simply hopeless. We enjoyed each other's conversations over the next few sessions. On the last day, I thanked her kindly for the suggestion of "Co-Dependent No More," a book I'd already tried to read twice. The work to be accomplished needed to be done by me. But I was single parenting, coaching a middle school field hockey team, and treading water financially until my legs ached when I crawled into bed nightly those days. The psyche work would have to wait.

I kept my children's last name until just recently. Had I changed it back to Read then, there would be more of that divorcee stigma I disliked. I used to think a mother with the surname Smith, who dragged around a couple of kids by the name of Brown, was a bit of a wild one who refused to give up her name at the time of the marriage. That, and I had plenty of trouble figuring out who belonged to whom on my hockey team as it was.

Moms who kept their maiden names while the children had dads last name on the register would come at me like, "Hi, I am Angel Smith, Aly Weidenberger's mom." I totally get the why, but sheesh it makes for a tough go getting the roster printed and laminated. Imagine fifteen or more players, with sometimes up to three hyphenated names, onto a three by five card, keeping them pocket-sized and all.

I wish now that I had had the wherewithal to be me then.

I told myself I would wait until my girls were out of high school to change my name or get a real job, which too could wait. My full time job was attempting to provide for my girls, while being at least somewhat present in their daily activities. The role of mother defined me in a new and brighter mode, belonging to A&A, as opposed to worrying about RR. My new friends saw just sunny and upbeat, strong and independent. A single mother thriving in the eyes of those who only saw me during daylight hours.

I cannot recall my parents planning around my sports events, nor worrying about getting to my school activities to spectate. My family will roll their eyes and tell you I turned out just fine even though they never attended a track meet.

I get it now, my parents had their own lives, jobs, yadda yadda. As you can clearly see/read, I am not fine. The idea of longing for acceptance or worth in the eyes of our parents is as old as time. I decided I'd be at every swim or track meet, hockey or lacrosse game, and school activity or field trip I could possibly manage. So maybe it's not our fault we are helicopter moms?

Back to that burning desire to write. For years I wrote press releases, articles about clients or their businesses, user manuals for techy computer stuff; informative pieces. "Clear and concise," my trusty motto. I cannot recall struggling to whip out a lengthy email, user guide, or compose descriptive brochure blurbs. I had no trouble explaining in text how your money might be safer with this financial planner rather than a big firm. Writing remained so simple when someone else's tale needed to be told.

My narrative has me doubled over in the gut, stopping to dry tears regularly. I am reliving pain, guilt and dreadful incidents which still have me convinced I am not worthy, in that quest for wholeness. Happiness is the holy grail of life, belief in ourselves as a valuable contributing member of society. Can you imagine Ellen on NBC saying "I just don't feel like I am doing enough?" Me either, but I heard her say it. Wow, have I got some work ahead of me.

Writing is so easy compared to designing and creating a logo that my client might use for the next 20 or 30 years. I am better at design and color schematics than I am at the art of text. An article for a weekly magazine, or the insignia an entire company will hang their reputation on? Symbols and lettering needed to be precisely veracious. The hundreds of hours of tweaking color, shape, font or even the name this new company will use from this day forward weighs heavy.

High stakes. Before launching a marketing campaign for a startup, printing five thousand brochures or one hundred screen printed tee shirts, you have to be sure you have a captivating logo. Once you roll out, there is no turning back on letterhead, web pages, advertisements or billboards. Geez, writing can be edited, why is this so difficult? And now with self-publishing, who can't write a book, easy peasy!

In the post office the other day, I told the attendant, "Yes, it's just that book again." You must verify it is only paper in order to get book rate mail postage for the package I was mailing. Saves about fourteen cents I bet.

The mail clerk in turn asked, "Oh is this the book you wrote and gave me last year?"

From about five yards out I hear, "Hey I am an author too, what's your name?" Very quickly, I shut that down. I turned to the nice elderly gal who was obviously eavesdropping.

"I am not a writer. Simply a mother who strung a bunch of nonsense into a paperback in hope of supporting the 'me-too' thingy."

"Well you're an author if you wrote a book," she declared.

I scooted out of the post office at hyper speed, only to get home to a very supportive email from Fitz stating, "$11.10 deposited into bank account from Amazon. I guess you're not only an author but a 'professional' writer." Laughing, I remembered a check for $30 in 1993 that made me a 'professional race car driver' too.

I am not an author. I am not a formally trained writer even. I am a middle aged person seeking renewed hope for transformation.

Years of therapy didn't work, and something's gotta give. I keep at this keyboard folks, still wondering where that sweltering desire comes from. Some say writing it down, getting it out, that'll help. I need the help. Storytelling Therapy.

This is maybe a bit late to mention that I do, in fact, envy those of you who write and author books as your means of income. What person wouldn't want to write prolific prose and get paid to ink out pages on some exotic island? Simply electronically shooting your product through cyber space to an agent through a laptop? Someone at the publishing house edits, formats, creates a whopper of a cover.

While there is envy, I am grateful that I do not have to count on "sales" for paying my rent or feeding my belly right now. That is pretty farfetched for my level of text. My burning desire to write is not to collect millions of dollars in revenue but to up my chances of survival psychologically. Maybe even become a better person, is that too grand an expectation?

Chapter 12

What happens if I don't write this book after all?

Coming clean is what people who have done wrong must do to clear their palate. Is my entire memory of the 50-plus years up until now just figments of my imagination?

Some days I ask myself, did anything really *that bad* happen to me which would require extensive therapy? Did I commit any true crime warranting waterboarding?

I feel like such a fraud saying I was abused or stalked or harmed in anyway. Especially when I blame some other being on this planet because, out of the other side of my mouth, I say I am the only one in charge of me. If I accept responsibility for my part in flying down the stairs, will I be able to forgive my father for aiding in the fall?

Am I somewhat responsible for antagonizing

the men in my life to harm me?

Good question, with a number of valid answers. Ask the men who did the deeds. They'll quickly confirm that I "got exactly what I deserved." Back talking. Mocking. Utilizing my super power of silence in the midst of a disagreement. I am quite good at shutting down.

Both of my exes can finger point with the best of them. While they continue to lie and cheat, it simply is no longer my problem. It does get me laughing though when I am feeling on top of my shit. Is it a crime to enjoy watching them high step through piles of manure?

When I could hear my mother seemingly fighting off my father – behind closed doors of course – did I feel partially responsible for getting her in trouble for something I did? Ah the child brain hopped up on "Catholicism." The only honest memory from those "loud nights on Briarcliff" is one where I wished I had never been born. The going was just too tough. Shutting down, turning off the brain, pillow over my head.

Side note: *that might be when I began to sleep more comfortably with the pillow on top as opposed to below my head!*

There was plenty of yelling at my best friend's house too, which made me feel better about my own surroundings. Her dad sometimes hauled off and hit her mom right in front of us kids, and the yelling was not reserved for just the bedroom.

My friend's dad often swayed in through the front door late evenings with crazy eyes and a horrible smell. I had no idea that it was alcohol stinking through his pores. We all just sort of grew up with the smacking and such. Nothing to see here.

I wonder now if the reason I felt like disappearing likely came from the fact that I was born the lesser gender. Certainly society sent glaring messages of women in the kitchen using the dish soap, and men smoking cigarettes on horseback, every girl subconsciously knew her place simply by watching the tube. The Read boys would follow in the family legacy of becoming terrific hockey players, I was simply a cheerleader.

It pained me to bother taking up space when all I would ever become is someone else's punching bag. No way was I ever going to have kids. I swore off of having children right up until I found out I was already fourteen weeks along with my oldest.

I can think of only one legitimate gripe I had during those years. The macaroni and cheese. At my bestie's house, her mother used real butter, and they always had the actual stuff in a bright blue box. Yes, I hereby declare Kraft tastes way better than A&P brand macaroni and cheese. Not in the way that a product endorsement will sway your purchase habits, but that one afterschool snack at the neighbors is what I recall as being superior. I honestly never noticed that I was a "have not" until later in high school. Hats off to my mom for that!

Forgive and forget? If I didn't speak up back then, shouldn't I be able to simply write out a short letter of forgiveness to those I begrudge and then let it go? I cannot take hearing one more person tell me that forgiveness is the only way to happiness. I know that for fuck's sake. It is deeper than that when you've spent all this time being angry. All these years ashamed of myself for what in fact was not anything I had control over.

With both girls on sports teams, I was around a lot of other parents on the daily. Yes, I envied the lovely mothers who handled crappy coach situations with grace and dignity. They kept their mouths shut about the game and smiled brightly even after a tough loss. How could I be more like them?

Yes, I wish I could have kept my mouth shut instead of yelling at the refs from the bleachers. Hello, that does no good and makes me the laughingstock!

Yes, I get that I am the most embarrassing mom on the planet. No, I am not proud of that fact. Yes, I wish I could change. No, people don't change, play the cards you are dealt.

Keep. On. Typing.

I am incredibly angry at myself for all of those years I didn't speak up for myself with my father, boyfriends, or husbands popping off on me. Sure, on occasion I hit back, or left their sorry asses, but the underlying anger is still inside of me. I know this because, when I try to talk about it, or write about it, my breathing quickens. I don't have high blood pressure, but I can only go at this a few pages at a time.

Anger only looks good on movie monsters. It's quite ill attractive on me.

Fellow team parents over the years would email electronic pictures of me on the sidelines at a game with a scowl or yelling. Not cool. If only we could get do-overs.

And just because I mention do-overs, would I take back any of those years of screaming from the bleachers? Yes, I think I would.

My mother attended a few games at the high school, and if that wasn't a shot of humility. Other parents would look over at us to see who it was making all the racket, and for just a slice in time, I was understood by a few of them. "Poor dear, I see where she gets it."

Yes, you don't have to ask. My oldest can be

heard a few blocks away from the field giving the ref, and sometimes the coach or opponent, her very loud and boisterous opinion. Dammit. *I can physically feel the Catholic guilt just typing that line.* I blame my mother for my cellulite for heaven's sake. Imagine what my girls can attribute to me?

There does come a time though when speaking up, stopping abuse, or bullying let's say, is the right thing to do. What nags at my brain is why do I think that I should be the one to speak up?

Plenty of other folks have been assaulted, ridiculed by Jane Doe coach, raped, assaulted or worse. I write a book about the way I see injustice permeating college sports, and am embarrassing my child by trying to get it out there. Both girls initially said, "Let it go Mom."

No one wants to be associated with the whistle

blower that's for sure, and because I have low self-esteem, I even question myself about the whistle.

If particular victims do not want to press charges, say players in their teens do not want to question the authority of the coach, who am I to say that any blowing needs the gust? I do believe that my teenage to twenty-year-old self did not have the proper tools though, which fuels my desire to speak up on behalf of young adults today.

Only recently have others begun to speak out and speak up about decades old assaults and such. It has allowed me the courage to write and give my childhood self a break – no one was speaking up, and it was happening to loads of girls.

Have you ever driven through thick fog or a snowy white out? Maybe a sandstorm on Highway 5 just outside of Bakersfield where 90 plus cars are piled up in one incident? It's scary because you cannot be 100% certain of what lies just yards in front of you. That is what living in fear feels like.

Imagine it, maybe not constant, but a dense fog flooding your existence quite often at the most inconvenient times.

Picture yourself crossing the street to avoid contact with unknown potential predators. Driving only in the daylight. Choosing only people or programs that you are familiar with so as to not have unexpected consequence or happenstance.

Panic, anxiety and fright well up at the drop of a feather somedays, no warning, just paralyzing me out of the blue. There is no telling how or why the bird phobia haunts me, but more than a handful of you have had to help me get the birds out of my house, out of my hair, or out of my cats' mouth because I simply cannot deal.

I eat the same thing every time I go out to dinner. I know what I like, and I know what I dislike. That's the easy stuff, feeding the belly. Feeding the mind is entirely different.

In order to make change, I must dive into the deep end – well, I am a great swimmer so not that – but cliff dive if you will into unknown territory.

Can I survive if I conquer the terror in my soul – that fear of being not worthy, stupid, ugly or inadequate, unfulfilled, not enough? Writing this stuff is scary, someone else reading it, terrifying. Potentially no one else will need to read this. I just keep writing until I feel better? Ha. That might mean forever.

Fear of rejection, ridicule, nonbelief. I question myself nearly every day about what I have done to be in this or that situation. Why do I feel so unfulfilled when in fact my girls are amazing, I live in a town I love, my apartment is cozy. Do I need more? No. Do I want more? Not exactly.

It's an itch really. Something nagging at my insides as if there are termites and, at any moment, the floor will cave. I'll fall in, be exposed as a phony, whining, no good, fraud of a human being with little or no drive to BE.

Bruises appear seemingly out of nowhere these days, so why do I give those childhood, or early marriage shiners, so much power over me?

Shut up and dance. Get over it. Move on. Live life with gratitude. Ef ef ef ef ef, why is this so hard for me?

Dammit, Joe Loya. In "Confessions of a Bank Robber," page 124, it says parents toss children down flights of stairs in all kinds of neighborhoods. No big deal.

Dammit Joe Loya. After reading his book, I

get it. *I can only control me, therefore forgiving my father for the abuse is entirely on me.*

I have spent so many years feeling this anger towards my father, and the next guy and the next guy. I'd bet good money that all the men who "wronged me" in my short lifetime are right now kicked back on their couches downing a beer or two in complete ignorant bliss. Fuckers.

For all the writing and journaling I've done on this topic to date, not much has changed. I allow the fear and anger to grow and accumulate mold in there until I can scrub it out with this "book".

Pause for dramatization here – shut down the computer to read a few pages of "The Lairs' Club" by Mary Karr. How exactly am I expected to keep going after reading something like that? She has real shit to unload on those pages. "Fuck this shit" keeps filling my thoughts, spilling out of my head, onto this page. I got nothing compared to Mary. Same with Joe. He fucking robbed banks. Of course I want to read his story. WTF.

Good news, this morning someone else in my group voiced similar concerns. Just keep typing because this is about me, for me, and needs to be completed by me in order to move forward.

Chapter 13

Siblings from same parents, different outcomes

There were three children in my family during the most tumultuous years, my sister came along later, when I was twelve. My older brother was a total hot head, the younger brother became a pot head. Do we have any scientific proof of how four children from the exact same two paternal adults can become night, day, evening and morning; east, west, south and north? We are all so incredibly different.

My oldest brother sulked around the house turning off the light switches. I've got no idea why just one of four children would be energy conscious.

I'd plug in the curling iron in the communal bathroom and head back into my bedroom to get dressed while it heated. Juice to the plug fueling the iron required the switch to be on in that room. I'd come back approximately 48 seconds, certainly less than a minute later, and the light would be off. Did he have an obsession with "conserving energy," or he just liked to get under my skin. I am not sure. He did it often enough that it's a "thing" I remember about him.

My bedroom light, the dining area light, even the porch light when habitants were not present seemed to bother him. When I say bother, anger rose up in his voice and eyes to the extent that I never challenged him on it, simply flipped it again, and went about my business. Older, stronger, he was a bit intimidating with his demeanor. Aside from hockey and his car, KISS (the band) was the only supplementary subject he seemed jazzed about. We were not close.

As I aged, I recognized an unbridled anger from within him that was daunting. Avoidance was my tactic. Never did he have anything nice to say to me. I recall continual criticism from him about my either "sucking up to teachers, parents, authority figures," or my being "stupid and ugly." We can get along well enough now, but he voted for the orange faced guy which really chaps me.

My older brother would become especially hostile if, or when, a team mate or pal of his at the house gave me any attention at all. You have to be able to put yourself in the body and mind of a young girl whose older brother's friends were "god-like" in order to understand what it was like between us. I worshipped his friends who were always "nice to me" as opposed to his continual loathing of me.

Because of the typical teenage angst and coming of age hormones, I was crazy about a number of his hockey buddies over the years. His dislike of me was palpable, and today I sort of get it. In a reverse, *protect the younger sister*, kind of way. It simply scared the crap out of me back then.

My approach to our relationship then, and

even sometimes now, is evasion. Wait for him to head down to breakfast before attempting any readying for school outside of my bedroom.

I was about 12, when he was 14, and he called me into his dimly lit bedroom. Nothing horrifying happened, but he did force me to touch his erect penis. It was not something I understood at the time and today am not directly nauseated by it, because that was the extent of the situation. I had to touch it.

For purpose of information herein, the freaking thing was huge. I mean, overly fertilized cucumber vs. banana in size. Rock hard. I was far too naïve to understand the situation, and backed out of the room quickly, not feeling "quite right" to stay. Bullet dodged knowing now what I didn't know then.

Things got pretty tense between us when he was forced to give me a ride to school a couple years later. My foggy brain will not allow me to pinpoint if I loved or hated getting a ride with him. With that line being so close, the love hate between us became a recurring theme.

My younger brother and I were very close. I felt like, being the older sibling to him, there was a somewhat more sound connection. The ever so slight feeling of being one to protect him from my older brother's anger and my father's wrath.

Ours was a house of cards if you will. Keep the peace so that no one gets hurt. Sure, I have read people's memoirs where guns and fires raged under their roofs in more elaborate fashion, but the noxious undercurrent was always in my gut.

My love hate relationship with my boyfriend in high school resulted in my younger brother being my escort during a homecoming event. I trusted him. He was a more malleable personality, with a nice girlfriend, and great potential to become a professional ice hockey player.

If the oldest is always the strongest, and the middle child sometimes gets lost in the mix, my younger brother was definitely the baby of the family, coddled and adored by all of us. Blond hair, blue eyes, nice guy. My older brother and I were brown hair, brown eyes, and the "milk man" question arose on occasion when the three of us were together in a room. Not until 12 years later when my blonde, blue-eyed, beautiful baby sister arrived, did all that subside. She took over as the baby, and things began to break down in many different ways on the home front.

For starters, my mother was hospitalized for a few days after the birth, so I remember kicking into high gear on diaper changing and bottle prep. My memory is nebulous, but I think I maybe got to stay home from school a bit to help out.

I was 12, making my brother just 10 when his role changed. By 14 we had formed a new bond being the middles, surviving the chaos of a life threatening illness where my father was hospitalized after a simple cyst removal. Only in this space, on this laptop, will I admit that I wished for my father to die from the procedure.

It was childish simple self-preservation musings of the beatings and yelling to subside, not the wishing him a horrible death kind of feelings. Those came later, after the infamous flight of stairs I tumbled down.

Back to my younger brother. He had moments where he actually defended me in a few dicey situations and, for those, I will always remember him fondly. While he is still with us physically, his charm and demeanor tarnished at about the time he started using drugs and alcohol. I don't have a pinpoint date for the beginning of the end, but I recently dug out a few letters he wrote to me from Switzerland in 1983. He had gone there after high school to refine his hockey skills.

While reading these long saved relics, I cried for the loss. He was a well-spoken, nice kid, on track to potentially skate in the NHL someday. Until the drugs. Tears well up. Do I miss him?

Am I angry at myself for not being more assertive at an intervention when he was younger? I wrote my letter with care, opening with something I liked, and maybe "missed" about my brother before drugs. I took care in writing, editing, and rewriting with mostly "the good stuff" shared with the closest siblings.

It should have worked. We were all gathered in some MSW's conference room, family, friends, the professional. Intervention was all the rage in the 80s, simple requirements such as all family and friends on board, each to prepare a little something in writing. This allowed, they explained, for less emotion so there was no overt anger or feedback expected from the fact that we all agreed it was time for him to get formal rehabilitation of some kind.

My brother was of course, shocked to find us all in one room together. I am pretty sure he was stoned, so that took the edge off by a bit.

"What the fuck, it ain't my birthday?" My brother, a witty and charming guy back then, stood as we are all seated in a semi-circle awaiting his arrival. The counselor invited us all to share what we had come up with in the form of letters to my brother, which went on for about twenty minutes. I don't remember who started, but I know who went last. My father.

"This is bullshit." My father said, being short on words, big on action. He pushed back his chair, grabbed my brother by the arm and exited before anyone else could speak.

We all sat in tears and disbelief. Who on earth allowed him in on this without vetting him? He was an absentee father in the first place, so what good would he be? A basic requirement of the intervention was that "all available immediate family members join in the mediation." Buggered.

If I am to try looking on the bright side, maybe this saved my mother from forking over the money for the transfer and housing because he certainly was in no condition to do the work, stay in any one place for more than a few days, and has not made a full recovery to this day. The addict has to want to go of their own will, or a successful outcome is bleak.

This refusing to cooperate by my father became an offense I could not forgive. The ignorant, abusive, highly influential "coach" in our community would rather watch his son fade to black than do the right thing.

We make excuses for this generation of males all the time. Forgive them, they were likely abused, or lived with addicts, or suffered some life trauma causing them to be ill- equipped to parent with any freaking common sense. The man had no reason to go against the rest of us aside from his ego. Bastard.

My compassionate younger brother is still in there somewhere, and shows flashes of empathy and kindness for children and animals he's watched over. He was a pseudo stepfather to a couple of children a few years back, and spoke about them with genuine concern on the few occasions I saw him. His cat of 15 plus years recently passed, and I was sad for him. Who is to blame when you are raised by such ignorance?

I wonder if he knows about that 15 year-old he used to care for having committed suicide a couple of years ago. I could not bring myself to ask, but threw a few dollars in towards the burial or whatever, broken hearted. The brother I knew and loved left me when he was 15, but in a different manner.

I have a sort of blanket over myself these days, where I only come out from under when I feel like there is enough light and warmth to sustain me. I don't like to be cold. I don't like feeling anger towards my father, or the sadness of missing my brother. I greatly dislike conversations with my mother where I end up feeling inadequate, a disappointment. I still hold her partially responsible as an enabler to my abusive father.

The family you are born to and raised by tugs at your heartstrings a few days per year around birthdays and holidays. We are not estranged per say, but I have kept my distance. Good friends are the clan we choose.

Working on me getting healthy does not allow

a shit ton of extra time or energy toward the people who are not interested in my getting better. My family will roll their eyes to nearly anything I have to say these days. Especially when I mention I am writing.

My older brother visited recently and, at the end of the visit, I felt the rolling of his eyes upon me. He sends subliminal messages of difference by saying, "Yeah, I grab a crotch or two, and the economy is great, so what's your problem with who is in office?" It took everything in my power not to slap him. Physical violence is in my DNA. The desire was almost overwhelming.

My brothers may or may not care to know that I have kept my girls at arm's length from them. The girls knew never to open the front door to my younger brother if I was not home. Drugs are unpredictable, and I always felt incredibly nervous around both brothers as we grew into adults. One has a short fuse, and the other, more often than not, is under the influence of this or that.

My girls are everything to me. The desire to protect them from growing up in any abusive situations is strong.

The fact that my values and actions differ from my siblings so greatly is still a mystery to me. All four of us from the same two biological parents. My siblings all agree that I am just a bit sour, or exaggerate the early abusive years a bit, and see no reason for alarm.

My reaction to sexual assault stories in the news certainly differs from theirs in that they have not lived my life. Same with the child abuse stories. None of them hit concrete at the foot of our basement stairs. I saw my brothers get the belt, or knocked around a bit, but boys deal with physicality on an entirely different level.

When someone says to me "you can only control you" over a cup of coffee, I tear up. Why do I have to be me? It's hard work, and it hurts inside. Am I wired wrong? It'd be much easier to simply let go of the demons in my mind and be more gracious, grateful, appreciative of what I do have. To be a girly girl and allow a man to take care of me, that's what I'll ask Santa for this year!

I do want to be a better person. I do fear my behavior will influence my children. I am trying.

They tell me writing all of this down in "memoir format" will help, by golly, I keep typing. Not happy about it, but something has got to change because I cannot continue in this angered state much longer. I am making every attempt to break the chain of violence in this lineage.

I got off track a bit when outlining the family dynamic. My incredibly smart, super cool, bubbly and attractive younger sister was of an entirely different generation and upbringing. My mother finally divorced my father in the 80s. She married the most intelligent, kind, handsome, and generous man I have ever known up close, when my sister was only seven or eight.

The mother my sister had in those formative years was recently college educated, emblazoned enough to leave the abuse, in love, financially subsidized, and on her way up out of the dark.

The two of them rented a house for a short time in between the divorce and new marriage. Seeing them on the wide porch of a Victorian styled rental house, with matching smiles, was bliss. A brighter future on tap for sure.

I was off trying to become an adult of my

own. Moving between Texas and Florida, they came to visit me in Bonita Beach one holiday. My stepfather was such a breath of fresh air. Smart, successful, loving, kind and generous.

Photos of all of us celebrating in the Florida sunshine are some of my favorite memories. My mother was a super skinny, peppy, renewed version of the woman I grew up with. My sister had this "happiness quotient" during middle school and subsequent private high school years to blossom under. I am genuinely happy for her. I can confidently say that I was blissfully happy being alone during the teen years with my girls, here's hoping it is enough to break the cycle of abuse.

Not wariness, but envy for sure resides in my soul over it. She was basically an only child to two adults in love, older and wiser as parents. Both my mother and stepfather had raised three children in the 60s and 70s, but this was a new day. A new relationship for each, and a chance to give my sister attention and time neither had had on the first go round. Really good stuff. It makes it very difficult for her to understand where I am coming from on issues of the day.

I was the beneficiary of this terrific stepfather for a few years when I returned to Michigan for college. He assisted in any way possible, an unconceivable force of a being. He was so good to my mother and my sister, with enough left over to counsel, support, and love me as well. A truly incredible man the likes of us may never see again.

I miss him greatly, I owe him dearly. The second time he helped save me was when I divorced the girls' dad. He was seven hundred percent there for my girls and me when we relocated from California to Michigan in 1997. The grandfather to my children that they, nor I, had never known, and the stepfather I needed during some pretty lean years.

Back to my sister. She is sunshine. The day and true North of four children born to our paternal parents. She is happily married, mother to two female future leaders, safe, and loved.

Not trying to be a martyr, I call myself evening and West in my earlier layout of us siblings. I am fun to be around most days. The oldest brother became morning and east, living a life of self-first. My younger brother dark of night, drugs pulling him south. He calls it free, says he is happy. All good.

The issue that has come to light of late, is the changing of my relationship with my mother and my sister. While I believe I am the same person I have always been – in great need of repair – they, in my eyes, have morphed into what I call "doctors' wives." I mean that lovingly, but the words have a sharp edge that can cut deep if I do not explain it properly. Here goes my attempt.

By marrying a doctor, you acquire a certain degree of financial security, a safety net if you will. You can usually get an Rx out of the deal in certain situations, that's huge. If or when doctor's wives divorce, there is a financial parachute of sorts.

The days I survived paycheck to paycheck, deciding whether to pay the phone or electric bill with the money I had, hardened me. A doctor's wife has tough days for sure, but not wondering if the next meal will include meat. The doctor is intelligent, employable, accomplished and of a fixed stature in society. Being that said guy or gal has acquired the M.D., he or she is more likely to be satisfied with themselves, presenting as a better partner to their significant others than say, for instance, me.

Friends and family have given me the business over the years about my not being fiscally responsible; no proper retirement plan, savings, or goals. Well, how about the fact that simply marrying a doctor has "provided" that big old bunch of security for some? Being married to a doctor was my mother's retirement plan? My friend married a doctor and was equally adamant about the fact that my lack of retirement planning was a huge issue. Easy for them to say right? Had I simply married a doctor, and stayed married for at least ten years, I too would be ready for retirement here shortly. Alas, I could not pull that off.

I dated a few doctors. I even had *potential* marriage proposals from a couple of guys who were gainfully employed as doctors or lawyers when we dated. I just am not cut from that same cloth. I cannot let someone else's earnings provide for me a sense of security.

Fitz says it all the time, "it's our money," but I disagree. If or when he leaves me, I tell inquiring minds I'll be out on the street corner with a sandwich board, "will marry for pension and benefits." What else have I got? I have supported myself for so long, been my own life vest and safety net, that the typical husband/wife scenario just seems to foreign. I am a giver, not a receiver.

I have trouble enough letting the good detective pay my rent – it plagues me with a sense of weakness to not pay my own way. Damn gallantry. It's not called that, but I have some sort of ridiculous ingrown hair of a mindset that tells me I must pay for something on my own for it to be "mine," or of earned value.

The only reason I am currently surviving the detective paying my rent is because I floated him a bit during his recent bankruptcy. Five years, in fact. We used my credit cards and stashed a bit of cash away during his situation, so now I tell myself that, for another three years or so, he can pay the rent and I don't have to feel guilty. Irrational thinking, but there you have it, my brain has a bit of crazy, just like number one, two and likely three would agree on. Girl is crazy.

A friend shared an article today about losing everything in a divorce, and staying afloat as a single parent. It is no easy feat folks. My story seems so unbelievable to people who cannot understand how, from my first two marriages, I paid them. Not making this up. The first one came out about forty grand ahead. The second one more than double that.

The first one asked that I put the equity from our house in to the children's names, then drained those accounts. I had failed to notice he was listed as "guarantor" on the AG Edwards accounts. Can you imagine a father stealing from his own children? Believe it.

Number two sued me for a crazy amount of money, telling a judge that half of RKC Marketing – a sole proprietorship / me – belonged to him. He was eventually awarded the house which was titled in both of our names, mortgaged in just mine due to his bad credit prior to our meeting. When he defaulted on the mortgage, guess what happened? Did anyone guess "he found another cash cow?" Yes, he did, and he bankrupted her too.

Forget it. That was a long time ago. But I did get my new friends here in San Luis laughing when I told them about the fund raiser I held. I tried to raise 186K by offering my marketing services at a two for one dollar price tag. Friends and family donated, I would commit double the money in logo, party invitation, party planning or marketing endeavors. I am still in arrears to some of you! I was not clear until later that I was having a full on nervous breakdown and trying to deny it!

The question has been raised on more than one occasion, "Why didn't you simply marry a doctor?" *Duh.*

Chapter 15

Martyr Pages – Why Me

During pity parties, while working on the question of "why me," I wonder these things:

Why do I feel responsible to right wrongs? Shut up and dance.

Why is nothing ever enough? I have so very much already.

Why do I believe that I am here for something greater than *this, what I am today*? Two successful happy children are proof that I did *something* right.

Why do I attract unwanted attention? Held up my pepper spray at a creeper yesterday.

Why am I writing in order to heal as opposed to simply getting back to being me? I was doing just fine before I decided to write this, or was I?

When I met number three I was self-sufficient,

happily planning my move to the west coast, on my own. What is different today?

I *know* happy, can throw fun parties and make people laugh, live with a sunny disposition in a very happy city, so why gripe? People like being around me.

Who do I think I am to worry about anyone on this planet aside from me? Let every "she too" stand up for herself and just work on fixing me.

Why the burning desire to write? I didn't go to writing school, nor do I spend much time honing skills necessary to write legibly.

When will enough be enough? Food, shelter, clothing, love – tons of people love me.

Can writing really heal a blemish or scar that is unidentified? This one is especially troublesome being that my immediate family will say that I am imagining a "wound." All is good.

Can I learn to love myself? That is a Biggy.

That is *the* Biggy. The Holy Grail if you will.

Am I deserving of love? Well, that depends entirely upon whether or not I can learn to love this jelly bellied over-the-hill body.

Why do I react the way I do? Folks say I could simply change my reaction to assault, battery, stalkers, creeps, birds. It is not that simple.

What is the proper response to assault? Kick him in the balls, fight back, play dead fish?

I read a recent news blip: "False accusations can cause people's lives to be shattered or destroyed." Well, what the heck do you think happens to victims and their family's people?

Chapter 16

Gender bias?

The male players in my life story to date have a unique ability to cordon off sections of their day, thoughts, actions and conscience with very little effort. They give attention to what matters most according to their upbringing.

Some strive for highest levels of education, others go for the almighty dollar, and there are some men who seek a balanced life with health, family, job and income. That balanced guy can keep the four themes safely in quarters that rarely conflict with one another. This is my observational breakdown, nothing scientific per say.

On the other hand, the women I know package and bundle thoughts, actions, goals, life purpose. If unwed with no children, there is the desire to support self, stay healthy, care for her siblings and or parents, contribute in her community, maintain a handful of friendships, and grow her mind in some way either through study, sport, or craft. If she finds herself on the path of motherhood, multiply all of the above by two or three depending upon if she attempts to have a happy healthy marriage, happy healthy children, and be a person too.

I am not trying to layout anything scientific, just point out my observations. My reflection is that women multitask and do quite a bit of juggling, while men take things more linear, one thing at a time.

I was pregnant prior to being married, so there was a fair amount going on with me from the get go. I had a full time job, with benefits to support the birth. The stigma of being pregnant and unwed while working in a male dominated oil industry is self-explanatory, no? Immediately my body, diet, thoughts and plans were altered by news of this pregnancy.

Had it been the flu, as I suspected and visited the doctor about, there would have been a one to two week pause in day to day activities.

I had no idea how much my life would change (yes, yes, yes, for the better) just as soon as my first child arrived. My baby daddy kept his usual schedule of work and biking and general "being," while I morphed into a sleep deprived, hormonal, sink or swim human, solely responsible for nourishing another person. That didn't last long, but where am I going with this?

Be aware. As a female, your daily to-do list is about fifty-eight items long. Males, about five. As a new mom, I juggled all of the pre-baby daily tasks, then took on responsibility for a whole other person. While I was finding day time care, working, breast feeding or keeping up on the laundry, this poor baby daddy was feeling neglected. Then he cheated.

Poor guy, his overweight and overly emotional new wife had very little energy left to pull off a proper striptease, or even allow dead fish sex after the day she'd had. Of course he cannot go without. He's a red blooded young man with a mind on one of four or five things. Sex, money, sex, job, sex, car, sex, hobby, sex.

The female engaged in baby making goes through some pretty effing major changes, obviously. I do not need to list the ways but should mention an entire body distortion, hormonal changes, lifestyle adjustment, etc. The male in many instances has played that pivotal role in creating the child, but is back at his old life within minutes of consummation.

No baby weight, food aversions, doctor visits, belly aches. On occasion you will hear about the dad bod, gaining a bit of sympathy weight, but in general males keep what they had in terms of body, temperament, schedule and or life style. Mine did. I have met some really terrific Mister Moms but that is not my story.

The women I know have strong moral compasses. The men I know believe themselves to be compasses. Ok, so he had one drunk driving and one PPO. He is *such a nice guy*. Sure, he has that sex addiction and slept with half a dozen babes he met online. He is a good provider, and *loves his children*. Big deal he beat his wife(s). He is up for promotion. *He is a good man.*

This whole "me too" movement is really causing a bit of distress for some, (not all), but "dangit ya'll," it is only "alleged abuse" at this point. Give a guy a break whydontcha? A guy date raped more than a dozen girls on the local campus, using ruffies, and was recently allowed to graduate after having been expelled over the incidents. Turns out, girls who have been drugged make less reliable witnesses in these cases. AND if you have the money, you can hire a big time Los Angeles criminal defense attorney after all is said and done to repair any damage to your curriculum in the dealio. Badda boom, badda bang, he's a college graduate!

If I hear one more orange faced comment about women being the liars. Well, no, nothing I can do about it but write. When the president of a country is a womanizing, cheating, lying, elected official, what does that say about our society? Yes, yes, of course, we can do better. I believe we will meanwhile.

A man will tell you it's not cheating if he didn't consummate. If they pull out, it doesn't count. If they do act, they have a "sex addiction" or some other "temporary insanity" explanation for us.

If some bitch gets all out of line, she needs

correcting by her man. Do I need to footnote the author of that, or can we just go with it? Again, based on my experiences, if you are still reading, you can see where I likely drove him to it, eh?

We used to find it entertaining to follow stories of "he said, she said." Today, as I type, shit's getting real. Men are losing their jobs, oh my. Due process? Show me one in fourteen thousand cases where the battered and bruised individual gets any justice.

I watched on television a father lunging at a monster who had molested three of his daughters. He was almost immediately tackled by four uniformed guards, as if he were the delinquent in the courtroom. Doggonit, I was hoping he'd have landed just one punch, on behalf of the hundreds of victims this *famous doctor* assaulted.

Victims rarely come forward, and the few that

do, seldom see legal justice served. In cases where he or she uses vigilante justice, the initial victim of a crime will spend their days in jail writing about this. I luckily never owned a gun. Therefore, am still typing out here in the free and clear. If memory serves me, a few strong women have "chopped it off" or shot their abusers and do time for it. Again, Lucky Me!

Chapter 17

A working woman

I have worked for companies large and small over the years. In roles as either employee or consultant, the harassment is consistent. As a consultant, I simply charged more for my time if I had to put up with an ass grab, or casual conversation over dinner about some guy's wife not putting out. I got rid of a few repeat offenders over the years, but marketing is a lot about selling, and selling requires a fair amount of schmoozing.

Harassment is not limited to large, small, private, public or government entities. Most studies show greater than fifty percent of working women have experienced harassment in one form or another, but only one in five report.

Nothing changes with the harasser if you report.

Nine times out of eight the reporter (i.e. me) ended up with the short straw – my study results. More often than not is what I am saying.

The couple of times when I did come forward against an assailant, I was in fear for my life, literally. The stalker guy got six months in jail. During that time I began to plan another get outta Dodge. If he "liked me" before, my best guess was a bit of time in the clink and he'd "really have it bad for me" upon his release.

Another gentleman was released from his job, at 52 years young, based on a report I filed. I see now how that could be a bigger problem than I originally understood, given it is tougher to find work after 50. I, who was only twenty eight at the time, was simply doing as I was told and scouting out locations. Sorry not sorry, he was breaking the law.

It was my supervisor at the time. A bigger boss asked me to drive out into the dessert east of Los

Angeles to verify a couple of addresses. Said supervisor threatened to kill me if I wouldn't change my report / findings about the fictitious locations for quick oil change shops. He, in fact, had a son in law who provided bulk tanks for said locations, so there was a double take going on. The bigger the corporation, the easier to skim a little here and there, eh? You can see why he, and potentially his son in law, wanted me out of the picture, no?

The most recent issue I had in a place of employment was especially creepy. The offender was never identified. I was less than a year in a job as a social media director when it became apparent that the company I was working for had zero intention of engaging in social media platforms. Odd it seemed to me, I was earning a hefty salary, though I was expected to do nothing, say nothing.

As I began to relay my concerns to upper

management, it became vividly clear that I was getting too nosey. Something fishy was up, I was to cash my paycheck and keep my mouth shut. When my then co-worker received a letter a few days before Halloween, it was short and sweet, typed in all caps:

YOU MAKE OUR GROUP LOOK BAD, WE DON'T LIKE YOUR KIND AT xxx!!!

J AND L SAID THIS COMPANY IS FOR GOD LOVINGAMERICANS; YOU AND THAT JEW RHONDA ARE ALWAYS CAUSING TROUBLE FOR US   GO BACK TO THE GHETTO AND TAKE YOUR N$%#&R LOVING SKINNY GIRL FRIEND WITH YOU

If not already stated, I am a recovering Catholic, but I've got a nose that some take for Jewish.

If you give the note a good look over, you'll see the word "skinny" and think it may be not all bad. When she and I sat down with the head of security, he explained that we ought to be vigilant in our comings and goings, remain on high alert.

I distinctly recall him suggesting we check our tires after a day in the parking garage because often time's angry folks slash tires. Very good bit of advice, we were terrified, teary eyed, and not at all comforted by this. I had been blissfully away from the corporate scene for nearly ten years at that point, and realized my mistake too late.

After a bit of this and that, meetings and memos, the company determined that "no hostile work environment" was in fact present. I was terminated from the company, with a small severance that would guarantee my silence.

I will quickly insert this. *Do not go to Human Resources if you have an issue with the company you work for. They exist solely to protect the company, not individuals.*

I was no longer a naïve twenty something. Now a seasoned veteran of work place harassment, I first attempted to simply relocate within the company. Nothing doing. Who wants a skinny girl in their department right? It was about four months later, ten days after an HR "investigation" found no evidence of hostile work environment, when I was relieved of my duties and escorted out of headquarters by the same security staffer who had counseled me on how to check my tires.

My termination pay check came only after my signature on a letter of silent compliance, I was to talk of this to no one, not the earlier hate mail, nor the severance. *Tee hee hee, I am now writing a "fiction novel" about the experience, great story, book three!*

Good riddance, both ways. I could go back to working from home, and use the severance to pay off some credit card debt I had accrued during the ten months of having no real work to do. (Insert online shopping a shit ton here.) I greatly disliked the way the company was functioning, and had done just fine as a self-employed marketing consultant, so what was the big deal?

The big deal ended up being my co-worker was also forced to leave. She did not deserve it. She had been with the company for years before my arrival. Adored by loads of folks at the company, she had started out as a trusted assistant to the founders. She had grown up with the company and worked hard to earn her position. She was just shy of being fully vested with her stock shares.

The women they brought in to replace us were a couple of super simple minded gals, former cable television *marketeers*, who likely would not challenge boredom. They came as a set, having both recently been fired from the local cable television company.

My co-worker and I both received multiple letters and memos after that first one, threatening us should we discuss the note, or its contents, with anyone from in or outside of the firm. We would be subject to a retaliation claim if so. Imagine how quick they flipped that we were the bad guys. Flushed out. There were some wrongs in there.

Maybe I reach out to her and we write the book about it together? Do I need to wait seven years? All good. It was nearly eight years ago. Say we write it, and they sue, great press for sales promotion, yes? Right, let's write!

It is about damn time to set records straight, believe one another, and pay equally based on merit; not gender, race, or other category. Don't make me pull this car over and beat you into understanding. Do watch for that fiction novel to come out next year where Ebony and Fiona go undercover to expose a lying, cheating, government conspiracy with that energy company.

Getting Back to Happy

Studies show, and it's quite obvious without research, that happy people are more better. I know that is bad English, but stay with me. More contented, better disposition. More amenable to relationships, better partners. More smiling, better looking. More of the good to better fend off the bad.

Along with the sunshine, there's got to be a little rain sometimes, and here, where I now reside, rain is cherished. Right along with the cliché line about rain, I'll add that all signs point to being in a happy, equal, authentic relationship requires a happy, healthy me first and foremost.

I have spent the better part of my days enveloped in low self-esteem. Imagine if this writing remedy helps lift me up ever so slightly. If I start to like me again, the possibilities are endless. Even if I do nothing different, doing what I do, a certain percent happier, makes a hell of a lot of sense. I refuse to settle.

Come on Rhonda, type the words, I AM WORTHY. (LOL. Spelled it wrong twice trying to type that worhyt, worhty.)

If I don't learn to love me, I will settle and stay stuck in the muddle of the past. I don't mean it as bold or controversial, but truthful. Feeling better already. Self-confidence cannot be overstated as being *the number one best gift* I can give myself after having done this exercise.

I read articles that state millions of people struggle daily with low self-esteem for one reason or another. If you are reading to this point, please consider taking pen to paper yourself. I was a true sceptic, made believer. I am not a writer, or an author, just me, working on being a better me. If just one person reads this, then calls to tell me they are getting a notebook started, I will be incredibly happy to the core! Email me at shetoobook at gmail dot com!

Call me corny, but it's time to be a bit more selfish and to start to love myself. Accept myself as I am, come to terms with the jiggly belly and the cussing, two things I do not see myself having power enough to change. But my reactions to life, the way I respond to the shaggy homeless guys tomorrow, I hope it's kinder.

This bank robber guy I met says he changed, maybe I can too. And if not, I now know a real live bank robber who might be able to give me some other tips, ya feel?

As I reflect on how life brought me to this place, there are only a few choice decisions I regret or would like as do overs. I imagine anyone in my position would have to admit to living in SLO being a huge step in the right direction of life. All I need to do is turn on the evening news and see fifty four car pile ups back home to know in my heart that I am in a better place now.

Getting some of the garbage out of my system and onto this page, liberating. Backyard bonfire can officially go on the calendar, burn it and move on.

Emotionally, I am still a bit of a train wreck when approached by Shaggy and Scooby down at the park, but I have my trusty gel pepper spray now. Physically, I can still enjoy a long walk along the ocean and appreciate the body I have been given, and, when I see bruises in the mirror, which is quite often of late, I laugh because I do not have any idea where they come from.

That is a funny thing right? I used to cry over the bruises, now I say what's the big deal with a few bumps along the way?

Spiritually I am still a bit of a waste. That Catholicism and the movie Spotlight have me like…"No thanks, not just yet."

Potentially I will head off on a trek across Spain or sign up for a meditation class when I finish this bit. Finances and Universe willing.

A few takeaways:

- Quit trying to outrun myself and accept me for who I am;
- Expect best versus fearing the worst;
- Keep my tribe small, only those who also accept me for who I am;
- Take a more active role in my decision making, don't settle;
- Write more, read less (just because the news of late is so depressing);
- Use happy words, a smiling face, and a positive approach to the day; and
- Forgive myself, stop chasing happiness and be happy.

AFTER WORDS

I wrote the previous pages a few months, and a few edits ago. Some early readers liked it, others wished it were more this less that. One even offered to recalibrate it to read chronologically, more upbeat, less self-doubt infused. Everyone has an opinion, and I am lucky enough to have friends willing to read my bits of truth so no complaining.

After a couple of recent weekends in San Francisco I have a few additional thoughts to pen.

Almost everyone I know talks to me about "back when." Back when she went to boarding school. Back when he met me in college. Back when the girls and I lived alone in a condo without anyone to answer to. Back when I lived in Ann Arbor, or worked at this job, or weighed way less. The update is I no longer want to look back.

I want to write. Write stories that matter

today, tomorrow, maybe even stories that highlight some of the "good old days" without rummaging up the dark. If people around me do not understand, so be it.

I will refer anyone willing to the Write or Die class offered by Anne Heffron in San Jose, CA. She'll travel to you if you can get four or more participants! Write your own story!

Being that the whole self-publishing deal allows for edits anytime, I will add also this story about my pepper spray.

A homeless guy grabbed my ankle in downtown San Luis a while back. He was pretending to be asleep outside of CVS on Marsh, and I really had not expected the grab. No harm no foul according to the police officer across the street, but I purchased my first hand held pepper spray that week. My daughter by my side, the clerk at the Army Surplus explained to me the difference between the gel versus spray, and its range. Get the gel folks, it's more direct, less chance for blow back!

I have carried it with me to the post office ever since, and when I visit San Francisco I almost always have it in my hand while walking. Did I already mention that my daughter went to Hastings, was attacked by a homeless guy? She suggested the pepper spray purchase a while back.

It was a terrific Mother's Day in San Francisco with my girls, which comprised of breakfast, cards, and the notorious RBG movie, capping with dinner out on Haight Street. Younger daughter and I were meeting a friend at Street Taco, but decided last minute that sangria at Cha Cha Cha sounded good. We were about ten blocks from her apartment.

Our fabulous dinner ended about 8:15 pm and we were headed home, on Haight headed towards Cole when the unthinkable happened. Unconceivable to my daughter and her friend who assured me, this never happens.

Two scruffy males walking towards us, used raised voices to demand money. First guy says "gimme all your money" and the second guy adds "gimme a dollar" as he pushes my daughters friend towards a building wall.

I am three feet to the left with my thumb on the pepper spray and reply, "that's why I have this," and a second warning, "this is why I have this."

The thugs were not listening, they had our male buddy two against one pushed up against a building when I made a direct hit to the side of the bad guys' face.

My first official depress on the hot pink thingy is a direct hit! I grab for both my daughter and her friend to run for it — will this guy recover from the blazing pepper and be more aggressive than a moment ago? I don't wait to find out.

Once our trio is safely across Haight, I notice a few onlookers and wonder why no one stepped up to help us. It is a total elapsed time of maybe seven seconds from start to finish of the encounter, and we are now three goofballs, doubled over in laughter about my antics.

Nervous laughter. Relief. Adrenaline pumped up me wondering how I pulled off the laser focused shot from my slightly crouched position, arms extended at the bad guys, barking out a fair warning.

After a few minutes to collect ourselves, I get a wee bit more serious. I lecture both of these two, who must from this moment forward promise me they will always have a compact in hand and at the ready on this boulevard plagued with known transients, hopped up on who knows what. I also assure them that it was probably just me, but then remind younger daughter that older daughter has already had her first encounter, that statistically it could happen to her.

I was so sure that having finished this book, I'd be a new person, less likely to attract the creepers because I am ten percent happier. Thank you Dan Harris' book. But doggone it, I am still me. Now one episode further into the life of RR, better keep writing!

Book Group Questions for Describing Water:

1. After reading this, do you think that your book might, in fact, be better?

2. Will you begin writing now, is there a book in you?

3. Was there a quote or line from the book that stood out?

4. Have you read memoirs before, and if yes, do you feel a connection with any?

5. Any feelings evoked by reading this?

6. Did the prose annoy you because it was not in any particular order?

7. Would you read a different book by this author?

8. Was the book too long, too short, do you have any suggestions for the author?

9. Any characters in the book that you could relate to?

10. Any places or settings in the book you could relate to?

Because I am simply writing this as narrative therapy, any and all comments are welcomed at mailto:shetoobook@gmail.com   Thank you! R Read

Made in the USA
Middletown, DE
06 September 2021

47688059R00139